NEW ENGLISH PAPER PIECING

A Faster Approach to a Traditional Favourite ● 10 Quilted Projects

SUE DALEY

C&T PUBLISHING

Text copyright © 2011 by Sue Daley

Photography and Artwork copyright © 2011 by C&T Publishing, Inc.

Publisher: Amy Marson

Creative Director: Gailen Runge

Acquisitions Editor: Susanne Woods

Editor: Karla Menaugh

Technical Editors: Teresa Stroin and Amanda Siegfried

Cover Designer: April Mostek

Book Designer: Kerry Graham

Page Layout Artist: Casey Dukes

Production Coordinator: Jessica Jenkins

Production Editor: S. Michele Fry

Illustrator: Aliza Shalit

Photography by Christina Carty-Francis and Diane Pedersen of
C&T Publishing, Inc., unless otherwise noted

Published by C&T Publishing, Inc., P.O. Box 1456, Lafayette, CA 94549

Library of Congress Cataloging-in-Publication Data

Daley, Sue (Sue Jennifer), 1956-

New English paper piecing : a faster approach to a traditional favourite--10
quilted projects / Sue Daley.

p. cm.

ISBN 978-1-60705-404-7 (soft cover)

1. Quilting--Patterns. 2. Appliqué--Patterns. I. Title.

TT835.D344 2011

746.46'041--dc23

2011022155

Printed in China

10 9 8 7 6 5 4 3 2 1

ACKNOWLEDGMENTS

To my wonderful staff, who always deliver and try to keep me focused—most of the time.

To Leanne Lawrence, who always manages to do an amazing job machine quilting my quilts with such short notice.

To Karla Menaugh, my editor, who was always waiting in the wings with the answers I needed.

DEDICATION

To my family, for all those years of understanding the meaning of the word *deadline*.

To my husband, Jim, for the constant support and help every step of the way.

To my four children, Ryan, Corey, Shannon, and Jarad, for being my biggest fans and for all your help over the years. Thanks for your understanding and support when my professional quilting life was so busy that I forgot to pick you up or was away for an important event in your life.

You have all contributed so much to enable me to work in a field that I love.

CONTENTS

Introduction

WE HAVE COME A LONG WAY

English paper piecing dates back to the early 1800s. While many beautiful designs could be created from the traditional hexagons, the process was very time-consuming. To begin a project, paper hexagons were cut from old letters or ledgers. Then each fabric shape, including a ¼" seam allowance, was cut individually with scissors. After the fabric pieces were thread-basted onto paper hexagons, they were whipstitched together. One quilt could take years to finish by hand.

Today the basic principles are the same, but technology has provided time-saving tools and materials for every step of the paper-piecing process. Today's patchworkers, with their busy schedules, can still achieve a handmade English paper-pieced quilt by using these time-saving tools:

- Basic precut paper shapes, available in many different shapes and sizes

- Acrylic templates with a built-in seam allowance, making it possible to rotary cut multiple fabric shapes at once

- Rotating cutting boards, saving steps in the rotary-cutting process

- A fabric glue pen, making it possible to replace time-consuming thread-basting with quick glue-basting; this tool alone cuts preparation time by at least half.

WELCOME TO MY WORLD OF ENGLISH PAPER PIECING

I was always turned off by how visible the whipstitched seams were on the front of English paper-pieced quilts. I was taught as a young child, "If you can't do it right, then don't do it." In my mind, those unsightly lines of whipstitching just weren't right.

When I switched to a thin, strong polyester thread, I found that I could solve two problems at once. The thread is so fine and strong that it sinks into the fabric, practically becoming invisible on the front of the quilt. And unlike cotton thread, it doesn't shred as it is being pulled across the top of the cards during the whipstitching process.

IT'S NOT JUST ABOUT HEXAGONS

Grandmother's Flower Garden is one of patchwork's oldest, dearest, and most frequently sewn designs. The design is based on a hexagon, which has six sides. In days gone by, these quilts were an allover pattern, made completely of hundreds and thousands of hexagons. Today you will still see people making these beautiful quilts.

Hexagon flower block

Detail of Grandma Rosie's quilt (page 93)

English paper piecing has predominantly been about hexagons, or occasionally six-pointed stars, octagons, or squares.

Today, English paper piecing can work with almost any shape. A wide variety of shapes, in many different sizes, will interlock just like a jigsaw puzzle. If the paper shapes fit together, their fabric counterparts can be sewn together.

There are endless possibilities! By combining my love of English paper piecing with my other passions, needle-turn appliqué and embroidery, I can introduce you to new possibilities for quilt design.

I combine appliqué with English paper piecing to create fresh, new looks for English paper-pieced projects. I have designed complex blocks that are made easy to sew by replacing difficult piecing with easy appliqué. And I have pieced graceful openwork designs that can be appliquéd to the quilt's background, also eliminating the need for difficult inset piecing.

By adding these approaches and the art of fussy cutting to English paper piecing, I hope to bring you into my world. You, too, can create beautiful quilts with these techniques.

Tools
&
Equipment

For information about where to buy the tools and equipment discussed in this section, see Resources (page 94).

FABRIC

All fabrics used for the projects in this book are 100% cotton unless otherwise stated. I prewash my fabrics. This is a good test for colourfastness. And if the fabric is going to shrink, it is better to have it shrink before you make it into something.

Choosing Fabric

Choose a fabric that you really love, and then pull all the colours from it. Always look past the obvious, and examine the pieces carefully to make sure you see all the colours. I always like to add something a little quirky, like a spot or stripe.

Two examples of fabric selection

When trying to reproduce an old scrappy quilt, you don't need to be so particular about matching fabric. Back in the 1800s, people did not have the luxury of patchwork shops, and they cherished every piece of fabric they had. If you want to achieve the antique scrappy look, almost anything goes.

Scrappy selection of fabrics

ROTATING CUTTING BOARD

I used to call this a luxury item, but now I call it a necessity. I use the Patchwork with Busyfingers boards, which allow me to turn the board as I rotary cut around each side of a template. The 10″ board is great for travelling or cutting on your lap. The 16″ is wonderful for using at home in your studio. I also use these boards while glue-basting the fabric to the paper shapes.

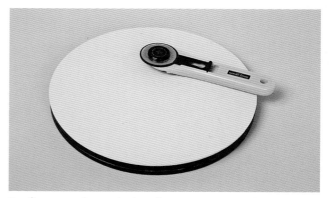

Busyfingers rotating cutting board

SANDPAPER BOARD

Perfect for tracing appliqué templates onto fabric, a sandpaper board will grip the fabric and keep it from moving while you trace. Place the fabric right side up on the sandpaper side of the board. Place the template on the fabric and trace around it.

TEMPLATE PAPER OR FREEZER PAPER

This is used for making appliqué templates. My preference is template paper, a heavy-duty tracing or drafting paper, because it is reusable.

THREAD

I use cotton thread with cotton fabric in most cases. The exception is when I am doing English paper piecing and needle-turn appliqué. Then my thread of choice is Superior Bottom Line thread. I use this in preference to cotton for English paper piecing because cotton thread shreds as it is continually pulled across the top of the cards during piecing. Superior Bottom Line is a strong, fine polyester thread that blends well and doesn't shred.

Superior Bottom Line thread

NEEDLES

I recommend a milliner's or straw needle in size 11, or size 10 if you prefer a slightly larger eye. The finer the needle, the finer your work will be. My preference is the Patchwork with Busyfingers size 11 needles.

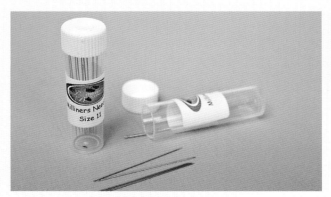

Busyfingers milliner's/straw needles

PAPER SHAPES

You can cut the shapes out of heavy paper, but if you want to save time you can use the Patchwork with Busyfingers precut paper pieces, which come in a variety of sizes and shapes. Packs include approximately 50 precut papers and an acrylic template for rotary cutting each fabric shape with the seam allowance. For large projects, when you need more than 50 precut papers, bulk packs are available. For information about where to buy the precut paper pieces, see Resources (page 94).

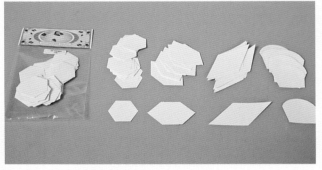

Busyfingers precut paper pieces

ACRYLIC TEMPLATES

I recommend the Patchwork with Busyfingers templates, which include the seam allowances. You can rotary cut around these through many layers of fabric on your rotating cutting mat. For information about where to buy the templates, see Resources (page 94).

Busyfingers acrylic templates

GLUE

Appliqué Glue

My glue of choice is Patchwork with Busyfingers Appliqué Glue. This glue is used instead of pins to attach appliqué shapes to the background fabric while you sew. It should be used sparingly, just a few small spots here and there.

Busyfingers Appliqué Glue

English Paper-Piecing Glue

The Sewline Fabric Glue Pen is ideal for basting the fabric to the paper shapes. Glue-basting saves so much time over thread-basting!

Sewline Fabric Glue Pen and refill

MARKING PENCILS

There are many marking pencils on the market. The Sewline Trio pencil has ceramic leads, and with one twist of the pencil you can change the colour of the lead.

Sewline Trio pencil

SCISSORS

Small embroidery scissors are ideal for snipping threads and cutting out small fabric shapes.

General sewing scissors are ideal for cutting larger pieces of fabric.

Paper scissors are used for cutting only paper, such as template paper or freezer paper.

BATTING/WADDING

For machine quilting, I recommend cotton or a poly/wool blend.

For hand quilting, I recommend a low-loft polydown.

English Paper-Piecing

Techniques

These instructions apply to all shapes when paper piecing.

1. Cut the fabric ¼" larger than the paper shape, all the way around. If you are using an acrylic Patchwork with Busyfingers template, fold the fabric into layers, place the template on top of the fabric, and rotary cut around the shape. For more information about templates, see Acrylic Templates (page 12).

2. Place each fabric shape wrong side up and place the paper shape on top, being careful to centre the paper shape.

3. Fold the seam allowances to the back of each paper shape and baste them in place.

Note

Some of the shapes, such as the hexagon, have corners that will fold in neatly. Shapes with smaller points, like the diamond, will have tails hanging out behind the point. Leave the tails hanging out, making sure that the fabric is basted tightly around the paper shape.

GLUE-BASTING METHOD

Using the Sewline Fabric Glue Pen to baste the seam allowances will cut your basting time about 75 percent.

1. Run the gluestick along one side of the paper shape, being careful not to get any glue on the fabric. (This would cause a buildup, making it difficult to stitch through.)

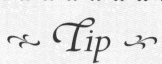

⁓ Tip ⁓

Don't use too much glue. In warm weather, the glue in the pen can become soft, making it easy to use too much. I suggest putting the pen in the refrigerator for a few minutes before using it.

2. Fold the fabric over and hold it for a moment. Continue around the shape until all sides are folded over.

3. When you are ready to remove the paper, just peel the fabric away. It's even easier than taking out thread-basting because you don't have the hassle of unpicking all the basting thread.

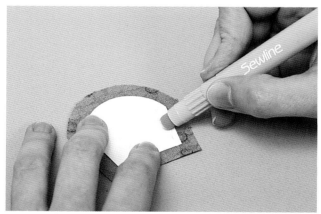

Glue application

ASSEMBLING THE PIECES

1. Place the right sides of 2 pieces together and whipstitch the seam from corner to corner. Start with a knot in the thread. Sew 2 or 3 stitches on top of each other to start. Taking small bites of fabric, sew with a whipstitch, approximately 16 stitches to the inch. Finish by making 2 stitches in the corner and overstitching 2 stitches back.

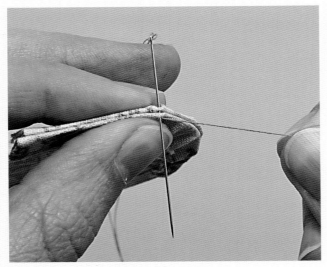

Beginning of the whipstitch

Whipstitch, 16 stitches to the inch

2. In most designs, you can sew pieces together in any order.

3. Open the pair. With a dry iron, give the set a press on the right side.

❧ Inset Seams ❧

Inset seams are easy with English paper piecing because you stitch only from corner to corner on each piece.

With right sides together, sew a seam with a whipstitch. When you get to the corner, just refold the pieces and realign the next edges you need to sew. English paper piecing helps you achieve perfect corners.

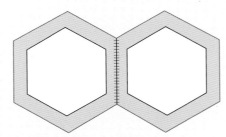

Hexagon paper-piecing assembly

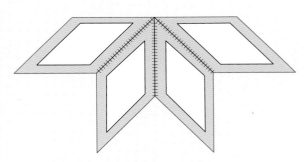

Eight-pointed star paper-piecing assembly

4. If you are making blocks that will be pieced to other blocks, you can remove the paper piece from each block as soon as it is surrounded and stabilised by other blocks. Press your work on the right side before removing the papers. The papers can then be reused a number of times.

5. If you are making blocks that will be appliquéd to a background, don't remove the papers until you are ready to appliqué. Press the block well, and then remove the papers. Using appliqué glue, baste the block to the background (Steps 1–4, page 17).

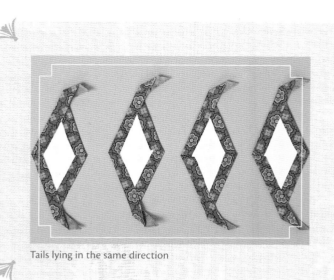

Tails lying in the same direction

NOTE

When sewing diamonds together, do not sew the tails in. Make sure the tails are all lying in the same direction at the points, and they will automatically lie flat behind your work.

When creating an eight-pointed star from 8 diamonds, sew the pieces into 2 halves and then sew the halves together with a single seam through the middle. This will prevent a hole from forming in the centre of your work.

Basting to a Background

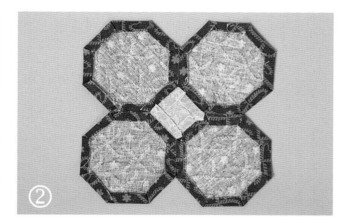

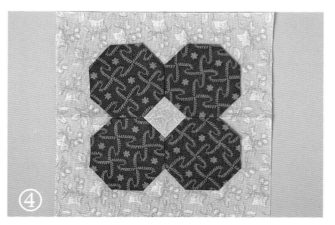

Removing the papers and placing the appliqué—Steps 1–4

FUSSY CUTTING

Fussy cutting—cutting a design element from your fabric for use in a specific location on a block piece—looks fantastic in English paper-pieced projects. Fussy cutting can add a whole new look to your work. But don't overdo it; remember less is more.

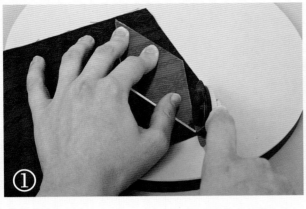

Fussy cutting—Steps 1–4

Step out of your comfort zone. Anyone can cut around a bird or a butterfly and centre it.

To make your block designs more exciting, choose an interesting fabric with a close pattern repeat. Place the template over the area you want to cut (1). Cut around the template with a rotary cutter (2). Place the cut fabric shape on top of the same pattern repeat on your fabric (3). Place the clear acrylic template on top, lining up the edges with the cut fabric shape (4). Using a rotary cutter, cut a second shape. Continue in this manner until you have the required number of shapes.

An example of fussy-cut fabric. See how placing the stripes in the same location on all the diamonds brings attention to the red squares? And the placement of the zigzag stripe in the orange fabric adds movement to the block.

Appliqué Techniques

GENERAL APPLIQUÉ INSTRUCTIONS

1. Always cut the background fabric ½" larger than the size it will be when pieced into the quilt. The outer edges of the quilt can fray, and the background can shrink a little when you appliqué or embroider on it, depending on how tightly you sew.

2. Make sure the design is properly centred. To find the centre of the background fabric, fold it in half and then into quarters. Lightly press the folds to mark the lines.

Fold the background fabric to find the centre lines.

3. Prepare the appliqué shape using your favourite method. If necessary, fold the appliqué shape in half and then into quarters to find its centre lines.

4. Using appliqué glue, place a few very small spots of glue on the wrong side of the appliqué shape. Match the centre of the appliqué design with the centre of the background fabric.

5. Stitch the appliqué to the background, using your favourite method.

6. Press the block and carefully trim it to the correct size.

NEEDLE-TURN APPLIQUÉ

For more information about selecting tools and supplies, see Tools and Equipment (pages 10–13).

Making Templates*

1. Place the template paper (heavy-duty tracing paper) over the design and trace. Alternatively, if your printer or copier will take this weight of paper, you can copy the shapes onto the template paper with this method.

2. Neatly cut out the template on the line.

* Instead of making your own templates, acrylic templates are available from Patchwork with Busyfingers. See Resources, page 94.

Preparing the Appliqué Shapes

1. Place the fabric, right side up, on a sandpaper board. This will keep it from slipping.

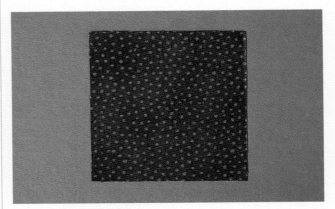

Fabric on a sandpaper board

2. Place the template on top of the fabric and trace around the edge.

Place the template on the fabric.

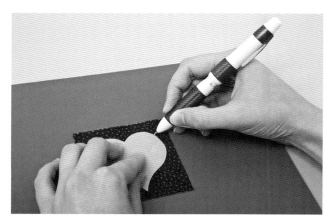

Trace around the template.

Drawn shape on fabric

3. Cut around the shape, adding a ³⁄₁₆″ seam allowance.

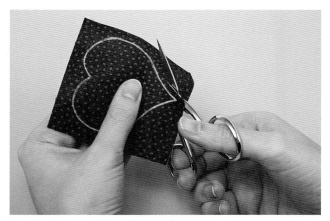

Cut the shape out with a ³⁄₁₆″ seam allowance.

4. Following the placement diagram, arrange the appliqué shapes on the background fabric.

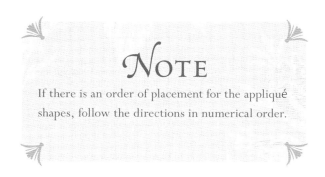
5. Use a few dots of appliqué glue to baste into position.

Place glue dots on the back of the appliqué shape.

Position the shape on the background.

To Clip or Not to Clip

* Straight edge: Do not clip.

* Outward curved edge: Do not clip.

* Inward curved edge: Clip to within 2 threads of the drawn line.

* Inverted point: Clip straight down 1 or 2 threads past the drawn line.

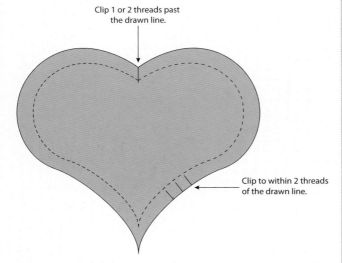

Clip 1 or 2 threads past the drawn line.

Clip to within 2 threads of the drawn line.

Sewing

⊱ Tip ⊱

If you are right-handed: Sew from right to left across the top of your work.

If you are left-handed: Sew from left to right across the top of your work.

1. Using a size 11 milliner's/straw needle and thin, strong polyester thread (such as Superior Bottom Line) come up from behind the appliqué piece just inside the drawn line.

Starting the appliqué

2. Making a scooping motion with your needle, tuck the seam allowance under so that the drawn line is hidden.

Scooping motion to turn under the seam allowance

3. Put the needle down into the background fabric right beside where the thread comes out of the appliqué piece. Keep the stitch close to the edge of the appliqué piece.

Needle straight down

4. Come up at an angle and take a small bite of fabric on the edge of the appliqué shape.

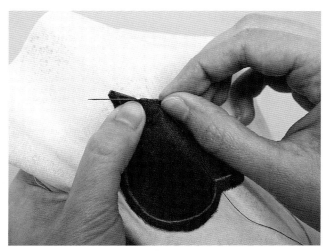

Come up at an angle.

Back of the work showing the stitch size

OUTER POINTS

1. Sew right up to the point. Turn your work around in your hands and do an extra stitch right at the point.

2. Fold the edge of the appliqué piece back and trim a small piece from behind.

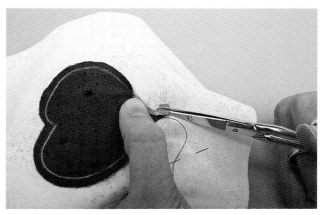

Cut away excess fabric behind the point.

3. Make sure that the seam allowance is only ⅛″ to ³⁄₁₆″ wide at this point, so the seam allowance will fit neatly into the outer point.

4. Fold the edge under.

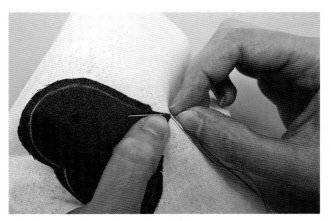

Fold the edge under and continue stitching.

5. Use the edge of the needle, starting about ½" further along, to scoop down to the point.

Scoop down to the point and continue stitching the second side of the outer point.

CURVES

Never clip an outward curve because it may create little points in the seamline. Make sure the seam allowance is not too wide, as this can also create little points on a curve.

1. For inverted points, sew right up to where you have clipped.

Sew into the point.

2. Sew 2 or 3 stitches on top of each other, taking a slightly larger bite of the fabric.

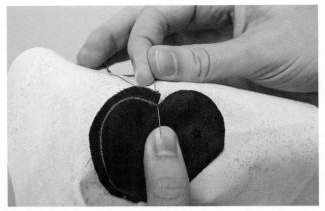

Sew 2 or 3 stitches on top of each other.

3. Continue on, turning the fabric under with your needle as you go.

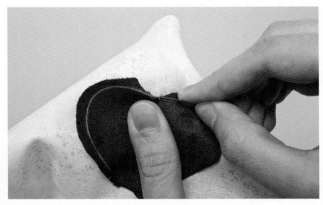

Scooping motion to turn under the seam allowance

Continue up the other side.

Completed appliqué shape

~ Tip ~

If you are getting little points on your curves, flick the fabric back out and realign the edge. No amount of sewing will get rid of the little points.

BIAS STRIP APPLIQUÉ

You can create a variety of stems, vines, and other linear design elements by cutting bias strips and folding their edges under with a bias tape maker. Clover bias makers are my favourite. They come in a variety of sizes and the instructions are on the product package. I use a ¼" Clover bias maker for this bias strip appliqué.

1. Cut a strip of fabric ½" wide on the bias.

Bias strip, ½"-wide

2. Feed the end of the strip into the bias maker, wrong side up.

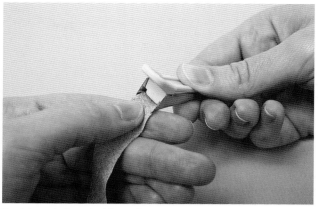

Feed the strip into the bias maker.

3. Pin the folded end onto your ironing surface.

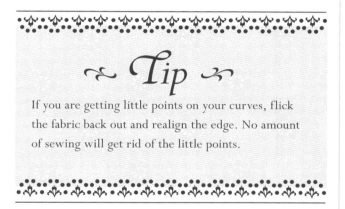

Pin to the ironing surface.

4. Keep the tip of the iron next to the bias maker as you pull it away.

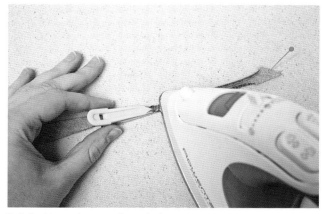

Pull the bias maker away from the iron.

The finished folded bias strip

5. Draw the design for the bias appliqué on the fabric.

Mark the design on the fabric.

6. Line up the folded edge of the bias strip with the drawn line on the background fabric.

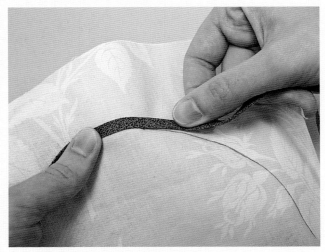

Placement of the bias strip on the background

7. Using a small appliqué stitch, sew the inside curve first.

Sew the inside curve first.

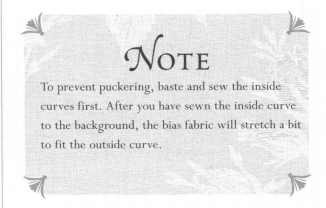

NOTE

To prevent puckering, baste and sew the inside curves first. After you have sewn the inside curve to the background, the bias fabric will stretch a bit to fit the outside curve.

BLANKET STITCH APPLIQUÉ

This approach is sometimes referred to as naïve appliqué. In this technique the raw-edge appliqué shapes are fused to the background fabric with fusible web. The raw edges are then covered by a decorative stitch that can be sewn either by hand or by machine.

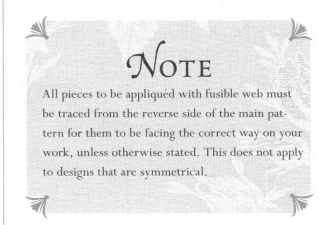

NOTE

All pieces to be appliquéd with fusible web must be traced from the reverse side of the main pattern for them to be facing the correct way on your work, unless otherwise stated. This does not apply to designs that are symmetrical.

1. Trace each design element onto the smooth side of the fusible web.

Trace the design.

2. Trim the fusible web to within ⅛" of the pencil line and iron it onto the wrong side of the fabric.

Trim the web and iron it to the wrong side of the fabric.

3. Cut out neatly on the pencil line with sharp scissors and peel the protective paper from the back.

Cut along the pencil line.

4. Place the shapes in the correct order on the background fabric and iron in place.

5. Stitch around the edge of each piece with a blanket stitch using 1 or 2 strands of embroidery thread.

Blanket stitch, sometimes called the buttonhole stitch

BLANKET STITCH

Come up at A. Hold the thread down and go down at B, then up at C.

Bring the needle tip over the thread and pull into place.

Finishing Your Quilt

BORDERS

When border strips are cut on the crosswise grain, piece the strips together to achieve the needed lengths.

Butted Borders

In most cases the side borders are sewn on first. When you have finished the quilt top, measure it through the centre vertically. This will be the length to cut the side borders. Place pins at the centres of the sides of the quilt top as well as in the centre of each side border strip. Pin the side borders to the quilt top first, matching the centre pins. Using a ¼" seam allowance, sew the borders to the quilt top and press toward the border.

Measure horizontally across the centre of the quilt top, including the side borders. This will be the length to cut the top and bottom borders. Repeat the pinning, sewing, and pressing.

Mitred Corner Borders

Measure the length of the quilt top and add 2 times the cut width of the border, plus 5". This is the length you need to cut or piece the side borders.

Place pins at the centres of both side borders and all 4 sides of the quilt top. From the centre pin, measure in both directions and mark half of the measured length of the quilt top on both side borders. Pin, matching the centres and the marked lengths of the side borders to the edges of the quilt top. Stitch the strips to the sides of the quilt top by starting ¼" in from the beginning edge of the quilt top, backstitching, and then continuing down the length of the side border. Stop stitching ¼" before the ending edge of the quilt top, at the seam allowance line, and backstitch. The excess length of the side borders will extend beyond each edge. Press the seams toward the borders.

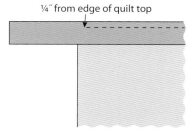

¼" from edge of quilt top

Start and stop stitching ¼" from the edge.

Determine the length needed for the top and bottom borders by measuring the width of the quilt top through the centre, including the side borders. Add 2 times the cut width of the border plus 5" to this measurement. Cut or piece the top and bottom border strips to this length. From the centre of each border strip, measure in both directions and mark half of the measured width of the quilt top. Again, pin. Start and stop stitching at the previous stitching lines, ¼" from the quilt edges, and backstitch. The border strips extend beyond each end. Press the seams toward the borders.

To create the mitre, place the corner on the ironing board. Working with the quilt right side up, place a border strip on top of the adjacent border.

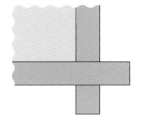

Border strip on top of the adjacent strip

With right sides up, fold the top border strip under itself so that it meets the edge of the adjacent border and forms a 45° angle. Pin the fold in place.

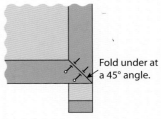

Fold under at a 45° angle.

Position a 90°-angle triangle or ruler over the corner to check that the corner is flat and square. When everything is in place, press the fold firmly.

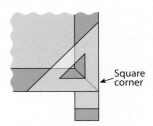

Square corner

Make sure the corner is square.

Remove the pins. Fold the centre section of the quilt top diagonally from the corner, right sides together, and align the long edges of the border strips. On the wrong side, place pins near the pressed fold in the corner to secure the border strips.

Beginning at the inside corner at the border seamline, stitch, backstitch, and then stitch along the fold toward the outside point of the border corners, being careful not to allow any stretching to occur. Backstitch at the end. Trim the excess border fabric to a ¼" seam allowance. Press the seam open.

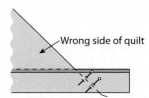

Wrong side of quilt

Stitch toward the outside edge for the mitred corner.

LAYERING AND BASTING

The method used will depend on the type of quilting that you prefer.

For Machine Quilting

1. Place the backing on a table, with the wrong side facing up, and tape it down. Mist sparingly with spray basting glue. See Resources (page 94).

2. Place the batting/wadding on top and smooth out. Spray lightly with basting glue.

3. Place the quilt top, right side up, onto the batting/wadding. Smooth out with your hands.

For Hand Quilting

1. Place the backing on the table, with the wrong side facing up, and tape it down.

2. Place the batting/wadding on top, smooth out, and tape down.

3. Place the quilt top, right side up, onto the batting/wadding. Tape it down. Pin or thread-baste all 3 layers together.

QUILTING

Some people have mastered the art of hand quilting and love doing it. Many love doing their own machine quilting. Others will have their work professionally quilted. Regardless of how it's done or by whom, quilting enhances the pieced or appliquéd design of the quilt.

You may choose to quilt in the ditch, echo the pieced or appliquéd motifs, use patterns from quilting design books and stencils, or do your own free-motion quilting. Remember to check your batting/wadding manufacturer's recommendations for how close the quilting lines must be.

BINDING

Trim the excess batting/wadding and backing so it is even with the edges of the quilt top.

If you want a ¼" finished double-fold binding, cut binding strips 2" wide and piece them together with diagonal seams to make a continuous binding strip. Trim the seam allowance to ¼". Press the seams open.

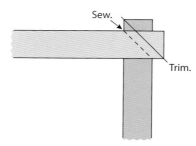

Sew from corner to corner.

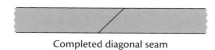

Completed diagonal seam

Press the entire strip in half lengthwise with wrong sides together. With raw edges even, pin the binding to the front edge of the quilt a few inches away from a corner, leaving the first few inches of the binding unattached. Start sewing, using a ¼" seam allowance.

Stop ¼" away from the first corner (see Step 1), and back-stitch 1 stitch. Lift the presser foot and needle. Rotate the quilt a quarter-turn. Fold the binding at a right angle so it extends straight above the quilt and the fold forms a 45° angle in the corner (see Step 2). Then bring the binding strip down even with the edge of the quilt (see Step 3). Begin sewing at the folded edge. Repeat at all the corners.

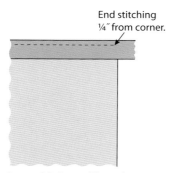

Step 1. Stitch to ¼" from the corner.

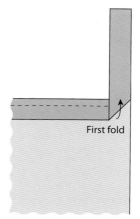

Step 2. First fold for the mitre

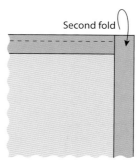

Step 3. Second fold alignment

Continue stitching until you are back near the beginning of the binding strip. See Finishing the Binding Ends (next) for tips on finishing and hiding the raw edges of the ends of the binding.

Finishing the Binding Ends

METHOD 1

1. After stitching around the quilt, fold under the beginning tail of the binding strip ¼″ so that the raw edge will be inside the binding after it is turned to the back side of the quilt.

2. Place the end tail of the binding strip over the beginning folded end. Continue to attach the binding; stitch slightly beyond the starting stitches.

3. Trim the excess end tail of the binding.

4. Fold the binding over the raw edges to the quilt back and hand stitch, mitring the corners.

METHOD 2

1. Fold the ending tail of the binding back on itself where it meets the beginning binding tail.

2. From the fold, measure and mark the cut width of the binding strip.

3. Cut the ending binding tail to that measurement. For example, if the binding is cut 2″ wide, measure 2″ from the fold on the ending tail of the binding and cut the binding tail to this length.

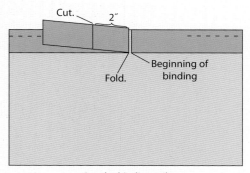

Cut the binding tail.

Open both tails. Place one tail on top of the other tail at right angles, right sides together. Mark a diagonal line from corner to corner and stitch on the line. Check that you've done it correctly and that the binding fits the quilt; then trim the seam allowance to ¼″. Press open.

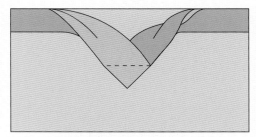

Stitch the ends of the binding diagonally.

Refold the binding and stitch this binding section in place on the quilt. Fold the binding over the raw edges to the quilt back and hand stitch, mitring the corners.

Projects

RINGS OF FRIENDSHIP

Made by Sue Daley, 2010; machine quilted by Leanne Lawrence

Made and machine quilted by Sue Daley, 2010

*T*hrough the years, many people have loved the Double Wedding Ring design for how wonderful it looks in scrappy fabrics and the romantic meaning of its interlocked rings. But piecing the arcs and curved seams using traditional methods is difficult and time-consuming.

Using pointed thimble shapes and English paper-piecing techniques makes this design easy to piece. By appliquéing the pieced arcs to the background fabric, you can eliminate the need for difficult curved piecing.

This pattern is ideal for anyone who would like to try a Double Wedding Ring design. It is such a fun project to make. It's not too big, and it will definitely dress up any bedroom.

BED RUNNER SIZE 19½" × 61½" | **CUSHION SIZE** 19" × 19"

ENGLISH PAPER-PIECING SHAPES

1" POINTED THIMBLES | 1½" SQUARES | ¾" HEXAGON FLOWER PETALS | ¾" HEXAGONS

Material Requirements and Cutting Instructions

You will need a paper and a fabric shape for each pointed thimble, square, hexagon flower petal, and hexagon in the quilt. Use the template patterns on page 40. Add a ¼″ seam allowance to each fabric piece.

For information on templates, see Making Templates (page 20).

Yardage	For	Cutting
1⅞ yards (1.7m) of tone-on-tone beige background fabric*	Bed runner: top	Cut 1 strip 20½″ × 62½″ on the lengthwise grain of the fabric.
	Decorator cushion	Cut 1 square 20½″ × 20½″. Cut 2 squares 20″ × 20″.
⅛ yard (10cm) each of 10 assorted red/coral fabrics	Bed runner and cushion: rings and flower centres	Cut 160 pointed thimbles: 128 for the bed runner and 32 for the cushion. Cut 6 hexagons: 5 for the bed runner and 1 for the cushion.
⅛ yard (10cm) each of 2 cream fabrics	Bed runner and cushion: rings	Cut 20 squares 2″ × 2″: 16 for the bed runner and 4 for the cushion.
⅛ yard (10cm) of light grey fabric	Bed runner and cushion: rings	Cut 20 squares 2″ × 2″: 16 for the bed runner and 4 for the cushion.
¼ yard (20cm) of grey/brown fabric	Bed runner and cushion: hexagon flower petals	Cut 36 hexagon flower petals: 30 for the bed runner and 6 for the cushion.
⅔ yard (60cm) of any fabric	Cushion: backing for the top (this fabric will not be seen)	Cut 1 square 20″ × 20″.
⅓ yard (30cm) of fabric (alternatively, you can use scraps)	Bed runner: binding	Cut 5 strips 2″ × the width of the fabric.
1¾ yards (1.6m) of fabric	Bed runner: backing	Cut in half from selvage to selvage. Seam horizontally to make a rectangle approximately 28″ × 70″.
28″ × 70″ of batting/wadding	Bed runner	
24″ × 24″ of batting/wadding	Cushion	
16″ cushion insert	Cushion	
Paper shapes for English paper piecing Template patterns are on page 40.		Cut 160 pointed thimbles. (*Optional:* 1 *Patchwork with Busyfingers* papers and template set plus 3 paper pieces packs)
		Cut 40 squares 1½″ × 1½″. (*Optional:* 1 *Busyfingers* paper pieces pack)
		Cut 36 hexagon flower petals ¾″. (*Optional:* 1 *Busyfingers* papers and template set)
		Cut 6 hexagons ¾″. (*Optional:* 1 *Busyfingers* papers and template set)

Requires a minimum usable fabric width of 41″.

CONSTRUCTION TECHNIQUES

Use a ¼" seam allowance unless stated otherwise. For information about cutting and piecing, see English Paper-Piecing Techniques (pages 14–18). To learn more about how to appliqué, see Appliqué Techniques (pages 19–27).

MAKING THE BED RUNNER

Ring Sets

1. Piece together 2 arc sections, each containing 4 pointed thimbles. Join the arc sections together with 2 squares to make a melon unit. Make 16.

Arc sections with squares
Make 16.

Melon unit

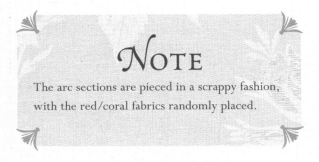

NOTE

The arc sections are pieced in a scrappy fashion, with the red/coral fabrics randomly placed.

2. Join the melon units to make a row of interlocking rings.

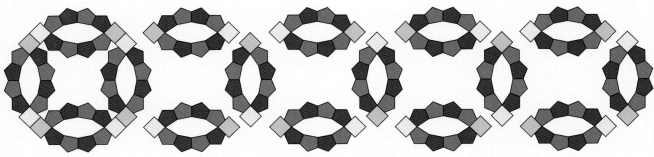

Join the melon units to make rings.

3. Press well on the right side.

4. Remove all the papers from the rings.

5. Mark the centre lines in the 20½″ × 62½″ bed runner background fabric by folding it in half in both directions and pressing lightly.

6. Place the background fabric flat, right side facing up. Make sure it is nice and flat.

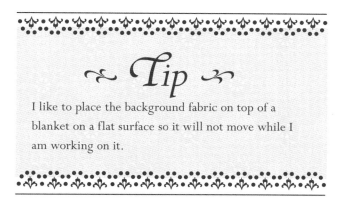

❧ Tip ❧

I like to place the background fabric on top of a blanket on a flat surface so it will not move while I am working on it.

7. Place the rings flat on top of the background fabric, making sure the set of rings is centred.

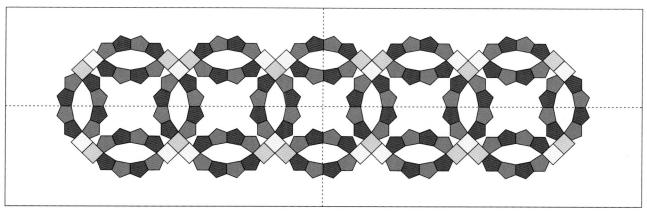

Centre the rings on the background fabric.

Note

It is crucial that the background fabric and rings be very flat at this point.

8. Working from the centre out, fold back a section of the rings at a time and apply a small amount of appliqué glue.

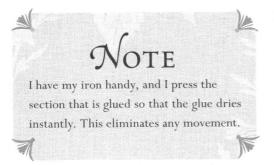
9. Continue until the entire piece is glue-basted into position.

10. Appliqué and press.

Hexagon Flowers

1. Piece the hexagon flowers using 1 hexagon and 6 hexagon flower petals for each. Make 5.

Hexagon flower
Make 5.

2. Press well on the right side.

3. Remove the papers and glue-baste a flower into the centre of each ring.

4. Appliqué and press.

Finishing the Bed Runner

Trim the runner to 20″ × 62″.

For information about how to layer, prepare for quilting, and bind your project, see Finishing Your Quilt (pages 28-32).

MAKING THE DECORATOR CUSHION

Ring Set

1. Following the steps for piecing the bed runner rings, cut and piece together 4 melon units to make a ring. You will need 32 pointed thimbles and 8 squares.

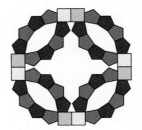

Pieced ring for the decorator cushion

2. Press on the right side.

3. Remove the papers.

4. Mark the centre lines in the 20½″ × 20½″ background square by folding it in half in both directions and pressing lightly.

5. Place it flat as described for the bed runner (Step 6, page 37).

6. Centre the ring onto the square and glue-baste into position.

Hexagon flower placement

Hexagon Flower

1. Make 1 hexagon flower using 1 hexagon and 6 hexagon petals.

2. Glue-baste and appliqué the flower into the centre of the ring.

Add the hexagon flower to the centre of the ring.

Finishing the Cushion

1. Trim the cushion top to 20″ × 20″.

2. Layer and quilt the cushion front. For more information about layering and quilting, see Finishing Your Quilt (pages 28-32).

3. Fold over an edge of a 20″ × 20″ square approximately ¼″ to the wrong side and stitch.

4. Fold the sewn edge over approximately 7″ to the wrong side and press.

5. Repeat Steps 3 and 4 on the remaining 20″ × 20″ square.

6. Place the cushion front on a flat surface, right side facing up.

7. Place 1 of the folded squares on top, right side facing down. Align the raw edges of the square with the raw edges of 1 side of the cushion top. The folded edge of the square will fall a few inches past the centre of the cushion top.

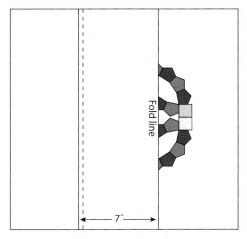

Cushion construction—Step 7

8. Place the other folded square, right side facing down, on top of the first 2 squares. Align its raw edges with the raw edges of the opposite side of the cushion top. The folded edge will overlap the folded edge of the square positioned in Step 7. This will create an opening at the back of the cushion to place the cushion insert.

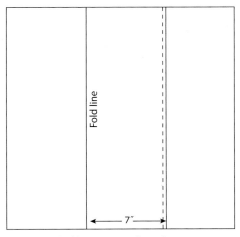

Cushion construction—Step 8

9. Sew around the outside edge of the cushion squares with a ½" seam allowance.

10. Clip the corners and turn right side out.

11. You can sew 2 buttons and buttonholes on the flap at the back, or use press studs or hook-and-loop fastener, such as Velcro.

12. Sew around the cushion cover, 2" from the outside edge, to create a flat border edge around the cushion.

Corner of the cushion showing the 2″ stitching line

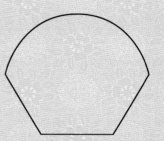

Template pattern for the pointed thimble

Template pattern for the hexagon flower petal

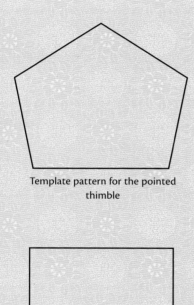

Template pattern for the square
(Use the square pattern for paper shapes only. Fabric squares are cut with the seam allowance added in the cutting chart.)

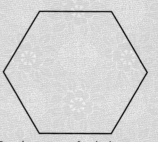

Template pattern for the hexagon

❋ Add a ¼" seam allowance to the fabric shapes but not to the paper shapes.

SQUARE DANCE

Made by Sue Daley, 2010; machine quilted by Leanne Lawrence

QUILT SIZE 65″ × 65″ | **FINISHED BLOCK SIZE** 13″ | **NUMBER OF BLOCKS** 13

. . . .

ENGLISH PAPER-PIECING SHAPES

2″ Curved octagon wedges | 2″ Diamonds | 2″ Squares

*V*ery often I start designing by just playing with paper shapes. This design started when I cut curved octagon wedges from a 2" octagon shape.

I knew that squares and diamonds would go with an octagon shape because of the size of the angles. So I moved the pieces around like a jigsaw puzzle until I had a design I liked.

Material Requirements and Cutting Instructions

You will need a paper and a fabric shape for each octagon wedge, diamond, and square in the quilt. Use the template patterns on page 45. Add a ¼" seam allowance to each fabric piece.

For information on templates, see Making Templates (page 20).

Yardage	For	Cutting
4⅜ yards (4m) of neutral fabric	Block background	Cut 13 squares 14" × 14".
	Border background	Cut 4 strips 13½" × 40".
39 fat sixteenths **or** 10" × 10" squares *Note: If you are fussy cutting, you will need more fabric.*	Full Square Dance blocks in the centre and corners	For each of the 13 full blocks, using a different fabric for each shape, cut: 4 curved octagon wedges. 8 diamonds. 4 squares 2½" × 2½".
Assorted pieces of fabric, approximately 6" × 6" square, to be combined with leftover fabric from the fat sixteenths or 10" × 10" squares	Partial Square Dance blocks in the border	For each of the 20 partial blocks, using a different fabric for each shape, cut: 2 curved octagon wedges. 2 diamonds. 1 square 2½" × 2½".
½ yard (40cm) of fabric	Binding	Cut 7 strips 2" × the width of the fabric.
4¼ yards (3.8m) of fabric	Backing	Cut in half from selvage to selvage. Seam horizontally to make a square approximately 73" × 73".
73" × 73" of batting/wadding		
Paper shapes for English paper piecing Template patterns are on page 45.		Cut 92 curved octagon wedges 2". (*Optional:* 1 *Patchwork with Busyfingers* papers and template set and 1 paper pieces pack)
		Cut 144 diamonds 2". (*Optional:* 1 *Busyfingers* papers and template set and 2 paper pieces packs)
		Cut 72 squares 2" × 2". (*Optional:* 2 *Busyfingers* paper pieces packs)

CONSTRUCTION TECHNIQUES

Use a ¼" seam allowance unless stated otherwise. For information about cutting and piecing, see English Paper-Piecing Techniques (pages 14-18). To learn more about how to appliqué, see Appliqué Techniques (pages 19-27).

MAKING THE SQUARE DANCE BLOCKS

1. Piece together 4 units, each containing 2 diamonds and 1 square. Connect these units with 4 curved octagon wedges to make a Square Dance block. Make 13. Press and carefully remove the papers.

Square Dance block

Make 13.

2. Mark the centre lines in each 14" × 14" background square by folding it in half in both directions and pressing lightly.

3. Appliqué a Square Dance block to a background square. Make 9 for the quilt centre.

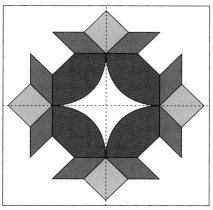

Square Dance block for the quilt centre

Make 9.

4. Appliqué a Square Dance block on point to a background square. Make 4 for the border corners.

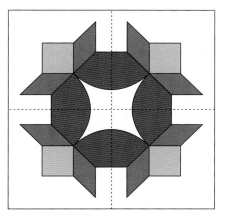

Square Dance block on point for the border corners

Make 4.

MAKING THE PARTIAL SQUARE DANCE BLOCKS

1. Piece a unit containing 2 diamonds, 1 square, and 2 curved octagon wedges to make a partial Square Dance block. Make 20.

Partial Square Dance block

Make 20.

2. Sew the partial blocks together in sets of 5. Make 4 sets.

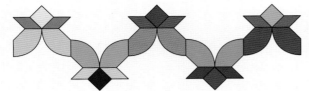

Partial Square Dance blocks set in groups of 5 for the quilt border

Make 4.

QUILT ASSEMBLY

1. Trim each of the 13 full Square Dance blocks to 13½" × 13½".

2. Sew the 9 straight-set blocks together in 3 rows of 3.

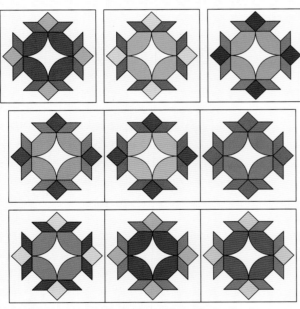

Centre block assembly

3. Press the 4 pieced border sets and carefully remove the papers.

4. Find the centre of each pieced border set by folding it in half in both directions and pressing lightly.

5. Mark the centre lines in the 4 border background strips by folding each in half in both directions and pressing lightly.

6. Match the centre lines of the pieced strips with the centre lines of the background fabric. Use appliqué glue (sparingly) to baste into position. Appliqué and press.

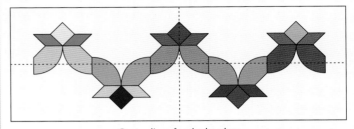

Centre lines for the borders

7. Measure through the middle of the quilt in both directions to check the measurements for the borders. The quilt should measure 39½" in each direction. Trim the border pieces to match the quilt.

8. Sew 2 of the borders to opposite sides of the quilt. Press well on the right side.

9. Sew a border corner block (one that has been appliquéd on point) to each end of the 2 remaining border strips. Press well on the right side.

10. Sew these 2 border strips to the remaining 2 sides of the quilt, lining up the seams. Press well on the right side.

Quilt assembly diagram

FINISHING THE QUILT

For information about how to layer, prepare for quilting, and bind your project, see Finishing Your Quilt (pages 28–32).

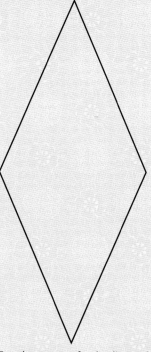

Template pattern for the diamond

Template pattern for the curved octagon wedge

Template pattern for the square

(Use the square pattern for paper shapes only. Fabric squares are cut with the seam allowance added in the cutting chart.)

❋ Add a ¼″ seam allowance to the fabric shapes but not to the paper shapes.

ICY NIGHTS

Made by Sue Daley, 2010; machine quilted by Leanne Lawrence

QUILT SIZE 53" × 53"

ENGLISH PAPER-PIECING SHAPES

1" POINTED THIMBLES | 1" SQUARES | 1" ELONGATED HEXAGONS

I just love the way the pointed thimble can be used to make so many different designs.

This shape will make a circle if you sew 16 together. Adding some simple appliqué changes the whole look of the quilt. The red petals in the centre of each pieced sections really brought life to this quilt.

I call this quilt size a bed topper. To decorate my bedroom, I often lay a quilt this size on top of a bigger quilt. You could also hang it on a wall.

Material Requirements and Cutting Instructions

You will need a paper and a fabric shape for each pointed thimble, square, and elongated hexagon in the quilt. Use the template patterns on pages 51. Add a ¼″ seam allowance to each fabric piece.

For information on templates, see Making Templates (page 20).

Yardage	For	Cutting
3⅛ yards (2.8m) of tone-on-tone beige background fabric	Centre block	Cut 1 square 33″ × 33″.
	Outer border	Cut 4 strips 8½″ × 59″ on the lengthwise grain of the fabric.
	Binding	Cut 6 strips 2″ × the width of the fabric.
⅜ yard (30cm) of taupe striped fabric	Inner border	Cut 4 strips 2½″ × 32½″.
⅜ yard (30cm) of red tone-on-tone fabric	Leaves	Cut 56 leaves.
	Cornerstones for the inner border	Cut 4 squares 2½″ × 2½″.
4 fat quarters of assorted fabrics ranging from pale to dark	Pointed thimbles	Cut 192 pointed thimbles.
	Elongated hexagons	Cut 16 elongated hexagons.
	Squares	Cut 72 squares 1½″ × 1½″.
3⅝ yards (3.2m) of fabric	Backing	Cut in half from selvage to selvage. Seam horizontally to create a square approximately 61″ × 61″.
61″ × 61″ of batting/wadding		
Paper shapes for English paper piecing Template patterns are on page 51.		Cut 192 pointed thimbles. (*Optional: 1 Patchwork with Busyfingers* papers and template set and 3 paper pieces packs)
		Cut 72 squares 1″ × 1″. (*Optional: 2 Busyfingers* paper pieces packs)
		Cut 16 elongated hexagons 1″. (*Optional: 1 Busyfingers* papers and template set)

CONSTRUCTION TECHNIQUES

Use a ¼" seam allowance unless stated otherwise. For information about cutting and piecing, see English Paper-Piecing Techniques (pages 14-18). To learn more about how to appliqué, see Appliqué Techniques (pages 19-27).

MAKING THE QUILT CENTRE

1. Piece together an arc unit containing 4 pointed thimbles and a 1" square. Make 24.

Arc unit
Make 24.

2. Stitch 10 arc units together with 8 elongated hexagons to make a row. Make 2.

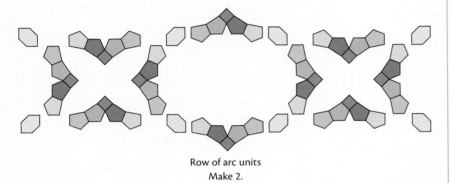

Row of arc units
Make 2.

3. Join the 2 rows with the remaining 4 arc units to complete the quilt centre.

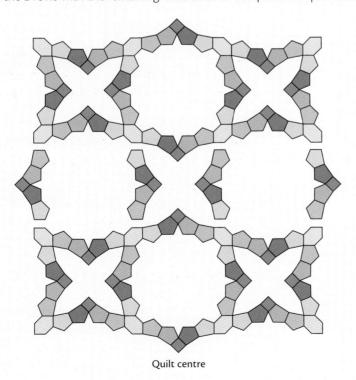

Quilt centre

4. Mark the centre lines in the 33" × 33" background square by folding it in half in both directions and pressing lightly.

5. Place the square flat, right side facing up. Make sure it is nice and flat.

> ### ⤳ Tip ⤳
>
> I like to place the background fabric on top of a blanket on a flat surface so it will not move while I am working on it.

6. Press and carefully remove the papers from the pieced section and place it flat on top of the background square, making sure the design is centred.

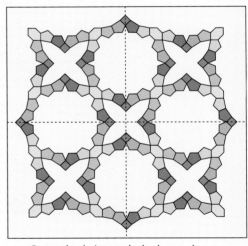

Centre the design on the background square.

> ### NOTE
>
> It is crucial that the design and the background be is very flat at this point.

7. Fold back a section of the design at a time and apply a small amount of appliqué glue.

8. Continue until the entire piece is glue-basted into position.

9. Appliqué into position and press.

10. Baste and appliqué the leaves, in sets of 4, onto the centre block.

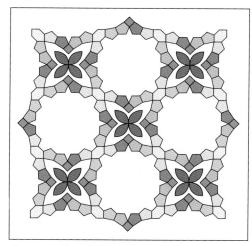

Placement diagram for the leaves on the centre block

11. Press and trim the centre block to 32½" × 32½".

INNER BORDER

1. Sew a 2½" × 32½" striped border strip to 2 opposite sides of the quilt centre.

2. Sew a red tone-on-tone 2½" × 2½" square to each end of the remaining 2 striped border pieces.

3. Sew these border strips to the top and bottom of the quilt.

Inner border

OUTER BORDER

1. Using all 4 of the 8½" × 59" strips, add a mitred border to the quilt body. For information about how to make a mitred border, see Mitred Corner Borders (pages 29–30).

2. Piece together 5 scallops, each containing 4 pointed thimbles and 1 pale square. Join the scallops together with 6 dark squares to make a border scallop set. Make 4.

Outer border scallop set
Make 4.

3. Piece together a border corner set containing 4 pointed thimbles and 1 pale square. Make 4.

Outer border corner sets
Make 4.

4. Sew the border scallop sets and border corner sets together to form a complete pieced border unit. For the border unit construction, refer to the border placement diagram (below).

5. Press and carefully remove the papers.

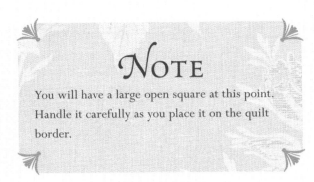

NOTE

You will have a large open square at this point. Handle it carefully as you place it on the quilt border.

6. Place the quilt in the same manner you used for the centre of the quilt, making sure everything is very flat.

7. Mark a faint line on the outer border 2¼" from the seam-line between the outer border and the inner border.

8. Place the pieced border unit on top. Make sure it is evenly spaced around the outside mitred border. Line up the bottom of each 1" × 1" square with the drawn line.

9. Glue-baste into position.

10. Appliqué and press.

11. Appliqué the leaves into position at the tips of the scallops.

Position border appliqué with base of square 2¼" from inner border.

Border placement diagram

FINISHING THE QUILT

Finished quilt layout

For information about how to layer, prepare for quilting, and bind your project, see Finishing Your Quilt (pages 28–32).

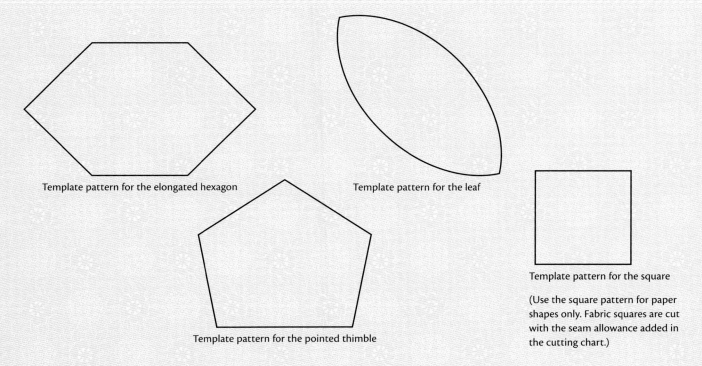

Template pattern for the elongated hexagon

Template pattern for the leaf

Template pattern for the pointed thimble

Template pattern for the square

(Use the square pattern for paper shapes only. Fabric squares are cut with the seam allowance added in the cutting chart.)

❈ Add a ¼" seam allowance to the fabric shapes but not to the paper shapes.

Shannon's Bag

Made and machine quilted by Sue Daley, 2010

BAG SIZE 10" × 13"

ENGLISH PAPER-PIECING SHAPES

2" ELONGATED HEXAGONS

*T*he inspiration for this bag came from my daughter, Shannon. For many years she had asked me to make a bag just for her. So while I was away teaching in Europe last year, I started piecing the elongated hexagons for the bag.

I especially love the colours of the fabric, which I collected while I was in Belgium.

Material Requirements and Cutting Instructions

You will need a paper and a fabric shape for each elongated hexagon in the bag. Use the template patterns on page 57. Add a ¼″ seam allowance to each fabric piece.

For information on templates, see Making Templates (page 20).

Yardage	For	Cutting
⅔ yard (60cm) of main fabric	Bag body	Cut 2 rectangles 15½″ × 12½″.
	Bag handles	Cut 2 strips 3″ × 30″.
10″ × 10″ square of green fabric	Stems	Cut ½″ bias strips to make about 26″ in total.
½ yard (40cm) of lining fabric	Lining	Cut 2 rectangles 15½″ × 12½″.
½ yard (50cm) of firm bag batting/wadding	Bag body	Cut 2 rectangles 16″ × 13″ (to be trimmed after quilting).
	Bag handles	Cut 2 strips 1″ × 30″.
8 squares 10″ × 10″ each of assorted fabrics (alternatively, assorted scraps)	Hexagons	Cut 36 elongated hexagons.
	Flowers	Cut 6 flowers.
Embroidery floss: pink and grey (Match these threads to the fabrics you are using.)	Flower centres	
Paper shapes for English paper piecing Template patterns are on page 57.		Cut 36 elongated hexagons 2″. (*Optional*: 1 *Patchwork with Busyfingers* papers and template set)

Other requirements

Clover ¼″ bias tape maker

Basting spray

CONSTRUCTION TECHNIQUES

Use a ¼" seam allowance unless stated otherwise. For information about cutting and piecing, see English Paper-Piecing Techniques (pages 14–18). To learn more about how to appliqué, see Appliqué Techniques (pages 19–27).

PIECING AND APPLIQUÉING THE DESIGN

1. Piece 18 elongated hexagons together, creating a staggered double-row unit. Make 2.

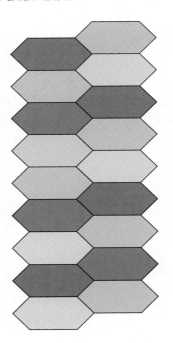

Elongated hexagon section
Make 2.

2. Press well on the right side.

3. Place the 15½" × 12½" rectangles of background fabric flat on a table.

4. Remove the papers from the pieced elongated hexagon units and position as shown. Glue-baste and appliqué.

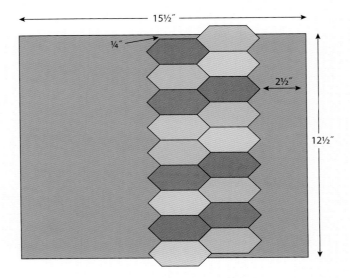

Placement diagram for elongated hexagons

5. Trim the tops and bottoms of both elongated hexagon units to align with the edges of the background rectangles.

6. Using the Clover bias maker, make a ¼" bias strip about 26" long. You will need to cut the strip to the required lengths for the appliquéd stems. (See Bias Strip Appliqué, pages 25–26, for instructions on using the Clover bias maker.)

7. Place the flower and stem appliqué elements on both background rectangles, following the numerical order in the diagram on page 55. Glue-baste and appliqué.

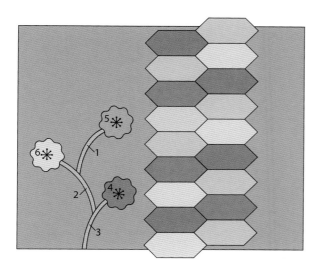

Order of placement and positioning diagram for the
appliquéd flowers and stems

8. Embroider the flower centres using a pistil stitch with 2
strands of embroidery thread.

Embroidering a Pistil Stitch

Come up at A and go down at B (point B becomes
the centre pivot of the stitch). Continue stitching
8 spokes, keeping them of equal length and
spaced evenly.

Add a French knot to the end of each spoke.
To make a French knot, come up at A and wrap
the thread twice around the needle. Holding
the thread taut, go down at B (as close to A as
possible, but not into it). Hold the knot in place
until the needle is completely through the fabric.

MAKING THE BAG

1. Layer the batting/wadding and an outside bag rectangle,
using basting spray to keep it in position while quilting.

2. Repeat for the other side.

3. Quilt as desired.

4. Trim the batting/wadding to the size of the bag
rectangles.

5. Place the 2 quilted bag rectangles right sides together.
Stitch a ½" seam allowance around the 2 sides and the
bottom.

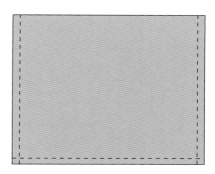

Joining the bag

6. To make the bottom corners into packet corners, fold
the bag so that a side seam runs down the centre. Measure
and sew 2½" in from the point. Repeat with the other side
seam and corner.

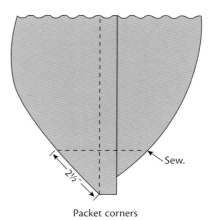

Packet corners

7. Trim off the point at each corner, leaving a ¼" seam
allowance.

Preparing the Lining

1. With right sides together, stitch the lining rectangles together in the same manner as the outer bag rectangles, including the packet corners.

2. Leave approximately 6″ open in the centre of a side seam. You will use this later for turning the assembled bag right side out.

Making the Handles

1. Fold the 2 strips 3″ × 30″ in half lengthwise to find the centre line, and then press.

2. Place each strip, wrong side facing up, on a table.

3. Spray lightly with basting spray.

4. Place a batting/wadding strip on top of each fabric strip, lining up an edge of the batting/wadding with the folded line.

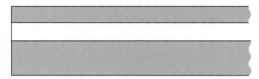

Batting/wadding placement on handle

5. Fold the narrower edge of the fabric over the batting/wadding so it is snug up against the edge of the batting/wadding (approximately ½″) and press.

6. Fold the edge of the other long side of the fabric over ½″ and press.

7. Fold again over the batting/wadding and press.

8. Make 2 rows of stitching down the length of each handle, each ¼″ from the outer edge. Make another line of stitching through the centre between the first 2 rows of stitching.

Top stitching on the handle

Assembling the Bag

1. Pin the handles into position on both sides of the bag, approximately 3″ from the side seams.

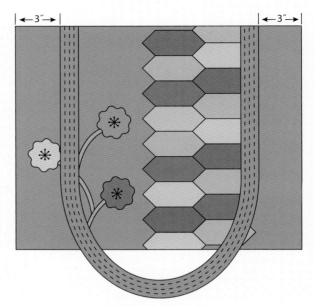

Handle placement

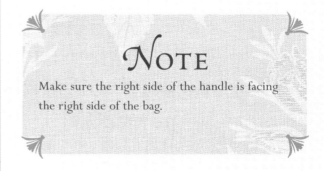

NOTE

Make sure the right side of the handle is facing the right side of the bag.

2. Turn the lining inside out and place the bag inside the lining, right sides together. Line up the side seams.

3. Pin around the top edge, making sure the handles are sitting straight.

4. Sew with a ½″ seam allowance all the way around the top of the bag. Turn the bag right side out through the gap you left in the lining side seam.

5. Sew the gap in the lining closed with a slip stitch.

6. Push the lining down into the bag. Make a line of top stitching approximately ½″ from the top edge of the bag. This will give a nice finish to the bag and keep the handles in position.

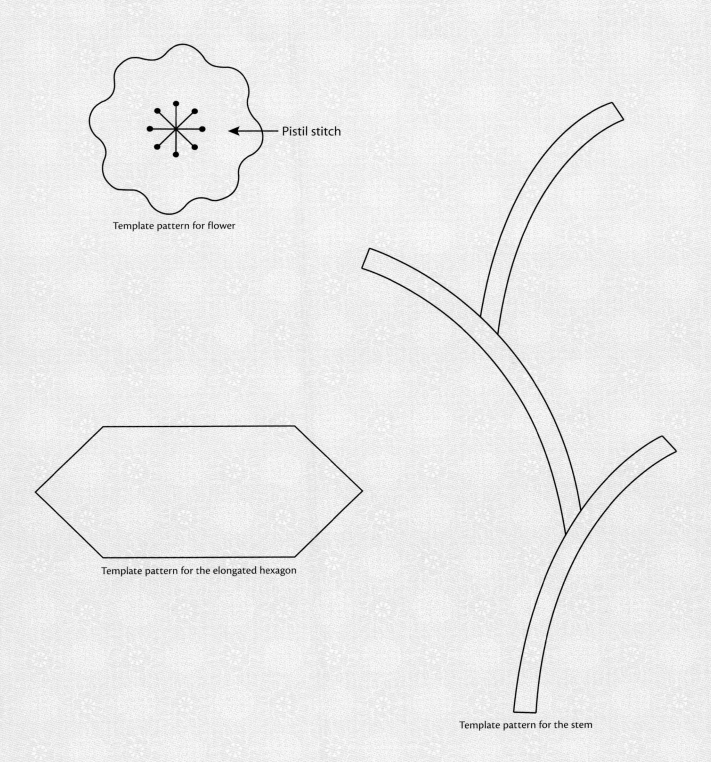

Pistil stitch

Template pattern for flower

Template pattern for the elongated hexagon

Template pattern for the stem

✼ Add a ¼" seam allowance to the fabric elongated hexagons but not to the paper ones.

JOINED AT THE HEART

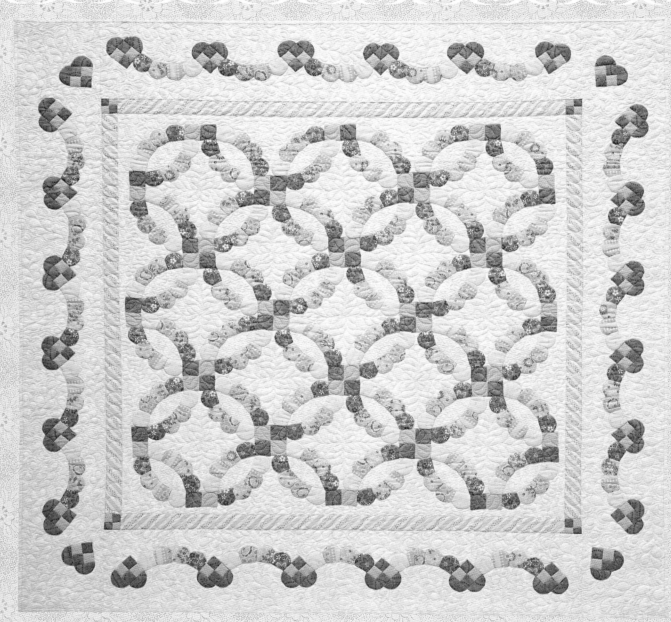

Made by Sue Daley, 2010; machine quilted by Leanne Lawrence

QUILT SIZE 60" × 60"

. . . .

ENGLISH PAPER-PIECING SHAPES

ROUNDED THIMBLES | 1½" SQUARES | 1" SQUARES | 2" HALF-CIRCLES

Material Requirements and Cutting Instructions

You will need a paper and a fabric shape for each rounded thimble, square, and half-circle in the quilt.
Use the template patterns on page 63. Add a ¼" seam allowance to each fabric piece.

For information on templates, see Making Templates (page 20).

Yardage	For	Cutting
3¼ yards (3m) of tone-on-tone beige background fabric*	Centre block	Cut 1 square 42" × 42".
	Outer border	Cut 4 strips 8½" × 45" on the lengthwise grain of the fabric. Cut 4 squares 8½" × 8½".
	Binding	Cut 7 strips 2" wide across the width of the fabric.
½ yard (40cm) each of 4 assorted blue fabrics, from light to medium	Centre block	Cut 288 rounded thimbles.
	Outer border	Cut 80 rounded thimbles.
½ yard (40cm) of dark blue tone-on-tone fabric	Centre block	Cut 36 squares 2" × 2".
	Inner border cornerstones	Cut 8 squares 1¼" × 1¼".
	Outer border hearts	Cut 56 half-circles. Cut 56 squares 1½" × 1½".
½ yard (40cm) of biscuit/caramel fabric	Centre block	Cut 36 squares 2" × 2".
	Inner border cornerstones	Cut 8 squares 1¼" × 1¼".
	Outer border hearts	Cut 56 squares 1½" × 1½".
⅓ yard (30cm) of striped fabric**	Inner border	Cut 4 strips 2" × 41½".
4 yards (3.6m) of fabric	Backing	Cut in half from selvage to selvage. Seam horizontally to make a square approximately 68" × 68".
68" × 68" of batting/wadding		
Paper shapes for English paper piecing Template patterns are on page 63.		Cut 368 1" pointed thimbles. (*Optional: 1 Patchwork with Busyfingers papers and template set and 7 paper pieces packs*)
		Cut 72 squares 1½" × 1½". (*Optional: 2 Busyfingers paper pieces packs*)
		Cut 112 squares 1" × 1". (*Optional: 3 Busyfingers paper pieces packs*)
		Cut 56 half-circles 2" (*Optional: 2 Busyfingers paper pieces packs*)

* Requires a minimum usable fabric width of 42".

** Requires a minimum usable fabric width of 41½".

My love of the Double Wedding Ring pattern inspired me to make this quilt. I was sitting quietly one day sketching some designs. There were some rounded thimble papers in a stack next to me. As I began to play with the shapes, suddenly the design was already done! I had the main shape, and I just needed to add the squares.

Sometimes designing can be that easy.

I love the colour blue but realized recently how seldom I use it. For this quilt my challenge was to use predominantly blue fabric, and I just love it.

CONSTRUCTION TECHNIQUES

Use a ¼" seam allowance unless stated otherwise. For information about cutting and piecing, see English Paper-Piecing Techniques (pages 14–18). To learn more about how to appliqué, see Appliqué Techniques (pages 19–27).

MAKING THE QUILT CENTRE

1. Piece together 8 rounded thimbles and 2 squares to make a melon-shaped unit. Make 36.

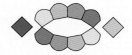

Melon unit
Make 36.

2. Join 4 melon units to make a Wedding Ring block. Make 9.

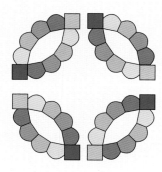

Wedding Ring block
Make 9.

3. Arrange the Wedding Ring blocks in 3 rows of 3. Stitch the blocks together, linked at the squares, to form the quilt centre. Press well on the right side and carefully remove the papers.

Quilt centre

4. Mark the centre lines of the 42" background square by folding it in half in both directions and pressing lightly.

5. Place the square flat, right side facing up. Make sure it is nice and flat.

Tip

I like to place the background fabric on top of a blanket on a flat surface so it will not move while I am working on it.

6. Place the wedding ring section flat on top of the square, making sure the unit is centred on the background.

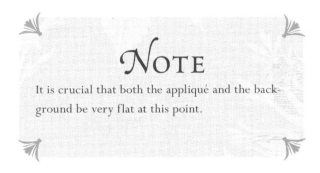

Note

It is crucial that both the appliqué and the background be very flat at this point.

7. Working from the middle out, fold back a section of the wedding ring unit at a time and apply a small amount of appliqué glue.

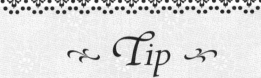

Tip

Have your iron handy. Press the section that is glued so that the glue dries instantly. This eliminates any movement.

8. Continue until the whole piece is glue-basted into position.

9. Appliqué into position and press.

10. Trim the quilt centre to 41½″ × 41½″.

ADDING THE INNER BORDER

1. Sew inner border strips to opposite sides of the quilt.

2. Stitch together 4 cornerstone squares to make a four-patch block. Make 4.

Four-patch border cornerstones
Make 4.

3. Press well on the right side.

4. Sew a four-patch cornerstone to each end of the remaining 2 inner border strips.

5. Press well on the right side.

6. Sew these 2 border pieces to the top and bottom of the quilt centre.

7. Press well on the right side.

ADDING THE OUTER BORDER

Mark the centre lines in the outer border strips by folding each strip in half in both directions and then pressing lightly.

Making the Pieced Outer Border Strips

1. Piece together 4 rounded thimbles into a swag. Make 20.

Outer border swag
Make 20.

2. Piece together 4 squares and 2 half-circles to make a heart. Make 28.

Outer border hearts
Make 28.

3. Join 6 hearts and 5 swags to make a pieced border strip. Make 4.

Outer border swag and heart section
Make 4.

4. Press well on the right side and carefully remove the papers.

5. Centre a pieced outer border section onto a border background strip.

6. Glue-baste the pieced border strip into position.

7. Appliqué around all the edges.

8. Repeat Steps 5–7 for the other 3 border sections.

9. Trim each outer border strip to 8½″ × 44½″.

Finishing the Outer Border

1. Sew 2 of the border strips to opposite sides of the quilt.

2. Appliqué a heart, on point, to an 8½″ × 8½″ square. Make 4.

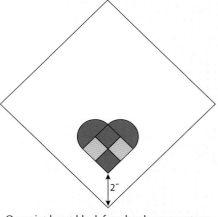

On-point heart block for a border cornerstone
Make 4.

3. Sew a cornerstone block to each end of the remaining 2 outer border strips.

4. Press well on the right side.

5. Sew the border strips to the top and bottom of the quilt.

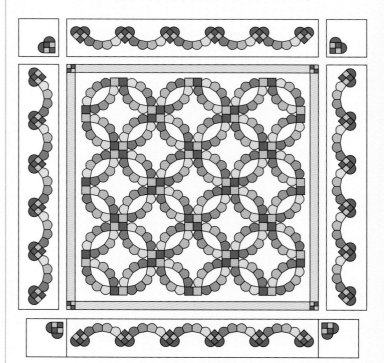

Quilt layout diagram

FINISHING THE QUILT

For information about how to layer, prepare for quilting, and bind your project, see Finishing Your Quilt (pages 28–32).

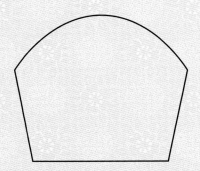

Template pattern for the rounded thimble

Template pattern for the 1½" square

(Use the square pattern for paper shapes only. Fabric squares are cut with the seam allowance added in the cutting chart.)

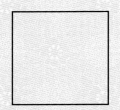

Template pattern for the 1" square

(Use the square pattern for paper shapes only. Fabric squares are cut with the seam allowance added in the cutting chart.)

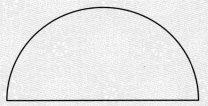

Template pattern for the half-circle

❋ Add a ¼" seam allowance to the fabric shapes but not to the paper shapes.

Time for Tea

Made by Sue Daley, 2010; machine quilted by Leanne Lawrence

TABLECLOTH SIZE 41″ diameter (approximately) | **NAPKINS SIZE (3)** 11¾″ × 11¾″

ENGLISH PAPER-PIECING SHAPES

¾″ HEXAGONS

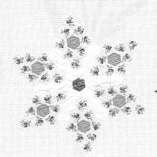

*M*y husband, Jim, and I own a bed-and-breakfast, where we often serve high tea to our guests. It seemed appropriate for me to design a tablecloth and napkins for high tea.

Material Requirements and Cutting Instructions

You will need a paper and a fabric shape for each hexagon in the tablecloth. Use the template patterns on page 72. Add a ¼" seam allowance to each fabric piece.

For information on templates, see Making Templates (page 20).

Yardage	For	Cutting
1¾ yards (1.6m) of background fabric*	Tablecloth	Cut 1 square 41" × 41".
	Napkins	Cut 3 squares 13" × 13".
	Hexagon star	Cut 18 hexagons ¾".
¼ yard (20cm) of light pink floral fabric	Hexagon star	Cut 48 hexagons ¾".
⅛ yard (10cm) of dark pink fabric	Lower butterfly wings	Cut 6 tablecloth lower wings and 3 napkin lower wings.
	Hexagon star centre	Cut 1 hexagon.
⅛ yard (10cm) of green tone-on-tone fabric	Hexagon star	Cut 6 hexagons.
¾ yard (70cm) of light green floral fabric	Upper butterfly wings	Cut 6 tablecloth upper wings and 3 napkin upper wings.
	Binding	Cut 2" strips on the bias to total approximately 142".
⅛ yard (10cm) of tan striped fabric	Butterfly body	Cut 6 tablecloth butterfly bodies and 3 napkin butterfly bodies.
Embroidery floss: tan, dark pink, light pink, and green (Match these threads to the fabrics you are using.)	Tablecloth embroidered border	
1⅜ yards (1.2m) of fabric*	Backing	Cut 1 square 41" × 41".
2⅜ yards (1.1 m) of stitchery stabiliser, 20" (90 cm) wide		
41" × 41" of batting/wadding (*optional*)		
Paper shapes for English paper piecing Template patterns are on page 72.		Cut 73 hexagons ¾". (*Optional:* 1 *Patchwork with Busyfingers* paper pieces set)

* Requires a minimum usable fabric width of 41".

CONSTRUCTION TECHNIQUES

Use a ¼" seam allowance unless stated otherwise. For information about cutting and piecing, see English Paper-Piecing Techniques (pages 14–18). To learn more about how to appliqué, see Appliqué Techniques (pages 19–27).

MAKING THE TABLECLOTH

Hexagon Star

1. Piece together 8 light pink hexagons and 1 green hexagon to make a diamond unit. Make 6.

Diamond unit
Make 6.

2. Piece together 1 dark pink hexagon and 6 background fabric hexagons to make a flower unit.

Flower unit
Make 1.

3. Piece together 2 background fabric hexagons to make a double-hexagon unit. Make 6.

Double-hexagon unit
Make 6.

4. Stitch the double-hexagon units to the flower's outer hexagons. Add the diamond units to make a hexagon star.

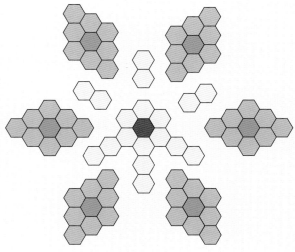

Hexagon star

5. Press from the right side.

6. Mark the centre lines of the background square by folding it in half in both directions and pressing lightly.

7. Place the hexagon star on the background, making sure it is centred.

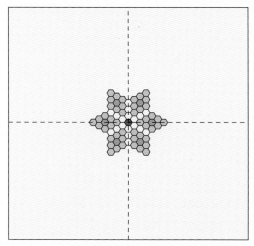

Placement diagram for centre star

8. Press carefully and glue-baste into position.

9. Appliqué in place.

Butterflies

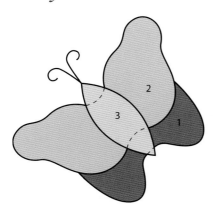

Order of placement for the butterfly pieces

1. Follow the placement diagram to appliqué the 6 butterflies onto the background fabric. The bottom of each butterfly body should be approximately 2″ from the cream hexagon in the centre star.

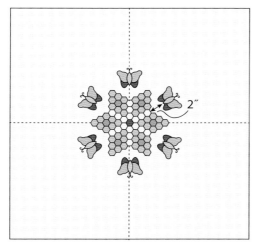

Butterfly placement diagram

2. Referring to the butterfly diagrams (above), draw the butterfly feelers onto the background fabric.

3. Embroider the butterfly feelers using 2 strands of embroidery floss and the stem stitch. To learn how to make the stem stitch, see Guide to Embroidery Stitches (page 69).

Embroidered Vine

1. To divide the tablecloth into 6 equal segments, fold the cloth in half through 2 opposite points of the star, and lightly press to mark the line. Fold in half through the other 2 sets of opposite star points and lightly press the lines.

2. Measure 11″ from each star point, out along the fold line, and mark. This will help with the placement of the embroidery line and cutting edge.

3. Trace the tablecloth edge embroidery scallop pattern (page 70) onto the cloth, beginning and ending at the points you marked 11″ from the star points. The embroidery scallop pattern repeats 6 times around the tablecloth.

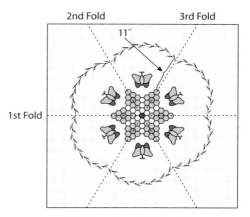

Folding and embroidery diagram

4. Iron the stitchery stabiliser to the back of the cloth.

5. Embroider; follow the tablecloth edge embroidery guide (page 70). To learn how to make the backstitch, colonial knot, and lazy daisy stitches, see Guide to Embroidery Stitches (page 69). Press.

Finishing

For my tablecloth, I quilted the front and backing together with an overall design just like a quilt, but without batting/wadding. If you decide not to quilt the tablecloth, the back and front need to be anchored in a few places.

1. If you are using a lightweight batting/wadding, layer the top with stitchery stabiliser, the light batting/wadding, and the backing fabric. If you prefer not to use a lightweight batting/wadding, layer the top with stitchery stabiliser and the backing fabric.

2. Using the tablecloth edge pattern (page 71), cut a scalloped edge around the tablecloth. The edge pattern repeats 6 times around the tablecloth.

Trim line diagram for the tablecloth edge

3. Using 2″ bias strips, make binding and apply it to the outside edge of the tablecloth. For instructions, see Binding (pages 31–32). Ease the binding in carefully as you sew around the scalloped edge.

MAKING THE NAPKINS

1. Appliqué a small butterfly to a corner of each napkin square, following the order-of-placement diagram on page 67. Place the butterflies at least 1″ from the napkin edges. Draw and embroider feelers for each butterfly.

2. Embroider 2 lazy daisies and 3 colonial knots to the other 3 corners of each napkin, at least 1″ away from the edges.

Detail of a napkin corner

3. Trim each napkin to 12½″ × 12½″.

4. Fold each edge over ¼″ to the wrong side and press.

5. Fold each edge again, ½″ to the wrong side, and press.

6. Topstitch around the outside of each napkin, ¼″ from the edge.

GUIDE TO EMBROIDERY STITCHES

Stem Stitch

Come up at A and then go down at B. In a short slanting stitch, come up at C (the midpoint of A and B). Repeat, keeping the stitches small and uniform.

To make a smooth, curved line, keep the thread length outside the curved line and bring the needle up inside the curve (C).

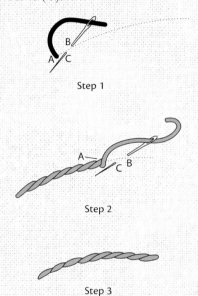

Step 1

Step 2

Step 3

Colonial Knot

Come up at A. Work the thread to form a figure 8–shaped loop, starting over the needle head and ending under the needle tip (Steps 1 and 2).

Hold the needle upright and pull the thread firmly around the needle. Insert the needle at B—as close to A as possible, but not into it (Step 3). Hold the knot in place until the needle is pulled completely through the fabric.

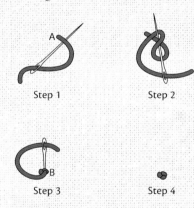

Step 1

Step 2

Step 3

Step 4

Lazy Daisy

Come up at A and form a loop. Go down at B (as close to A as possible, but not into it); then come up at C, bringing the needle tip over the thread (Step 1).

Go down at D, making a small anchor stitch. (Steps 2 and 3).

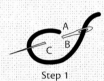

Step 1

Step 2

Step 3

Backstitch

Come up at A, take a small backward stitch, go down at B, and then come up at C (Step 1).

Going back down at A, move the needle forward under the fabric and come up 1 stitch length ahead (D), ready to take another stitch (Steps 2 and 3).

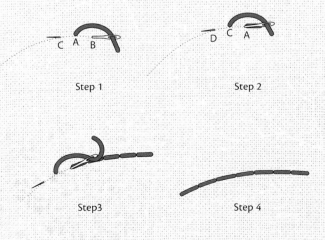

Step 1

Step 2

Step 3

Step 4

To create the full scallop: Trace the pattern, and then move it to the right, aligning the template join lines. Trace again.

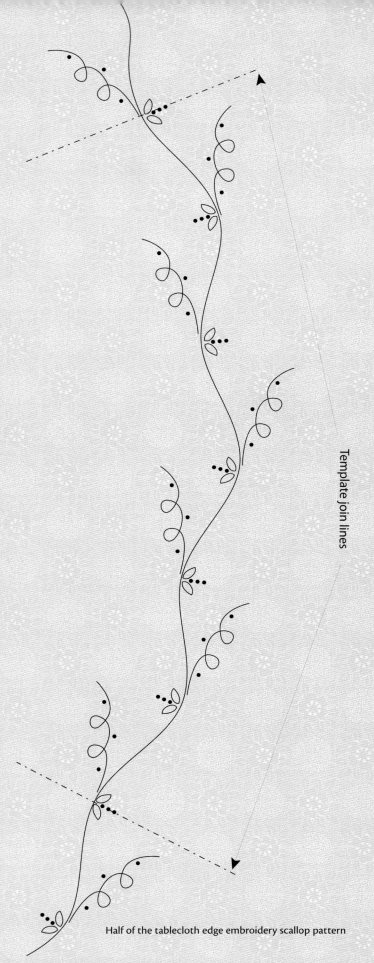

Template join lines

Half of the tablecloth edge embroidery scallop pattern

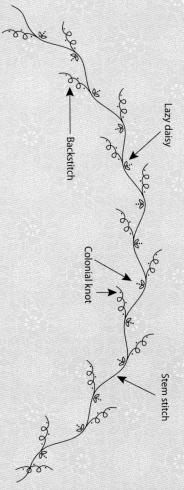

Lazy daisy

Backstitch

Colonial knot

Stem stitch

Tablecloth edge embroidery guide

Align with paper fold.

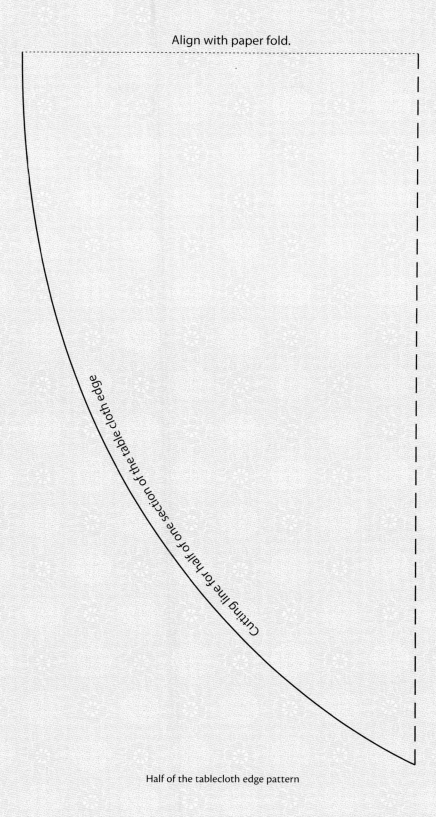

Cutting line for half of one section of the table cloth edge

Half of the tablecloth edge pattern

❋ To create the full pattern: Fold a 15″-long piece of paper in half crosswise. Align the short edge of the pattern with the fold in the paper. Trace the pattern. Cut on the traced line and unfold the paper.

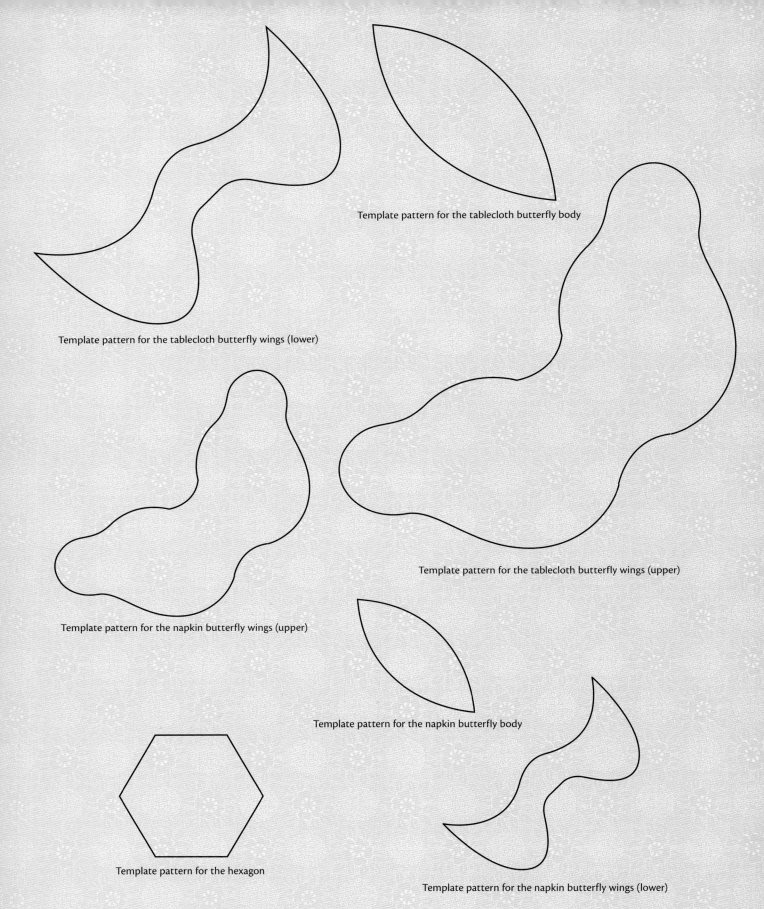

Template pattern for the tablecloth butterfly body

Template pattern for the tablecloth butterfly wings (lower)

Template pattern for the tablecloth butterfly wings (upper)

Template pattern for the napkin butterfly wings (upper)

Template pattern for the napkin butterfly body

Template pattern for the hexagon

Template pattern for the napkin butterfly wings (lower)

❋ Add a ¼″ seam allowance to the fabric hexagons but not to the paper ones.

WELLINGTON

Made by Sue Daley, 2009; machine quilted by Leanne Lawrence

QUILT SIZE 66" × 66" | **FINISHED BLOCK SIZE 9⅛"** | **NUMBER OF BLOCKS 12**

ENGLISH PAPER-PIECING SHAPES

2" JEWELS | 1" DIAMONDS | 1" HEXAGONS

Material Requirements and Cutting Instructions

You will need a paper and a fabric shape for each jewel, diamond, and hexagon in the quilt. Use the template patterns on pages 80–82. Add a ¼" seam allowance to each fabric piece.

For information on templates, see Making Templates (page 20).

Yardage	For	Cutting
3⅜ yards (3m) of cream tone-on-tone fabric	Swag border*	Cut 4 strips 8½" × 60" on the lengthwise grain of the fabric.
	Star blocks	Cut 2 strips 10" × the width of the fabric. Subcut into 6 squares 10" × 10".
	Checkerboard centre and border	Cut 9 strips 3½" × the width of the fabric. Subcut into 93 squares 3½" × 3½".
2¼ yards (2m) of black tone-on-tone fabric	Star blocks	Cut 2 strips 10" × the width of the fabric. Subcut into 6 squares 10" × 10".
	Checkerboard centre and border	Cut 9 strips 3½" × the width of the fabric. Subcut into 92 squares 3½" × 3½".
	Swags	Cut 20.
2 yards (1.8m) of border print fabric with dark and light variations	First border*	Cut 4 strips 2" × 24". Cut down the length of the fabric, making sure the strips are on the same pattern repeat.
	Star blocks	Fussy cut 36 jewels. Cut on the same pattern repeat on the light part of the fabric.
	Star blocks	Fussy cut 36 jewels. Cut on the same pattern repeat on the dark part of the fabric.
	Binding	Cut 8 strips 2" × the width of the fabric.
1 yard (90cm) of red fabric	Second border	Cut 4 strips 1½" × the width of the fabric. Subcut into 2 strips 1½" × 36½" and 2 strips 1½" × 38½".
	Centre appliqué	Cut 1 small medallion.
	Star blocks	Cut 72 diamonds.
	Swag border	Cut 20 fleurs-de-lis.

*For most efficient use of the fabric, cut these lengths first.

chart continued on page 76

Yardage	For	Cutting
	Centre appliqué	Cut 1 large medallion.
⅜ yard (30cm) of brown fabric	Swag border	Cut 20 circles.
	Star blocks	Cut 12 hexagons.
4¼ yards (3.9m) of fabric	Backing	Cut in half from selvage to selvage. Seam horizontally to make a square approximately 74" × 74".
74" × 74" of batting/wadding		
Paper shapes for English paper piecing Template patterns are on pages 80–82.		Cut 72 jewels 2". (*Optional*: 1 *Patchwork with Busyfingers* papers and template set and 1 paper pieces pack)
		Cut 72 diamonds 1". (*Optional*: 1 *Busyfingers* papers and template set and 1 paper pieces pack)
		Cut 12 hexagons 1" (*Optional*: 1 *Busyfingers* papers and template set)

*T*he ratio of males to females in my family is 4 to 2, so the pressure was on to create a masculine quilt.

I have always loved black and tan as a colour combination, and a touch of red was a perfect addition to this quilt. I used the art of fussy cutting to showcase the fabric.

And, of course, a strong-coloured quilt needed a strong name, so Wellington was my obvious choice.

Having made the quilt to satisfy the men in my family, I was informed a while ago that it is my daughter-in-law Jules's favourite quilt!

CONSTRUCTION TECHNIQUES

Use a ¼″ seam allowance unless stated otherwise. For information about cutting and piecing, see English Paper-Piecing Techniques (pages 14-18). To learn more about how to appliqué, see Appliqué Techniques (pages 19–27).

CENTRE CHECKERBOARD

1. Using 13 cream squares and 12 black squares, stitch together 5 rows of 5 squares each. Three rows should begin and end with a cream square. Two rows should begin and end with a black square. Stitch the rows together, alternating the colours, to create the centre checkerboard.

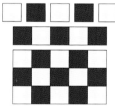

Centre checkerboard

2. Press well on the right side.

3. Appliqué the medallion pieces to the pieced block, making sure they are centred.

Centre block appliqué

FIRST BORDER

Using the 2″ print border strips, add a mitred border to the centre block. For information on making a mitred border, see Mitred Corner Borders (pages 29–30).

Centre block and first border

ENGLISH PAPER-PIECED BLOCKS

1. Cut and piece together 6 jewels, 6 diamonds, and 1 hexagon to make a star unit. Make 12.

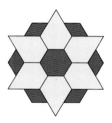

Star unit
Make 6 with light jewels.

Star unit
Make 6 with dark jewels.

2. Press well on the right side.

3. Mark the centre lines in the 6 black and 6 cream 10″ × 10″ squares by folding them in half in both directions and pressing lightly.

4. Remove the papers from the paper-pieced stars and glue-baste into position on the black and cream squares.

5. Appliqué the stars to the background squares.

Finished star blocks

6. Press the blocks and trim to 9½" × 9½".

7. Stitch a black star block to a cream star block. Make 2 sets.

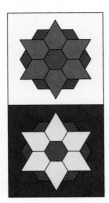

Star set
Make 2.

8. Sew a star set to either side of the centre checkerboard unit, with a cream block on top on the left side and a black block on top on the right side.

Checkerboard centre with side stars

9. Sew 2 cream star blocks and 2 black star blocks together in an alternating pattern to create a star strip. Make 2.

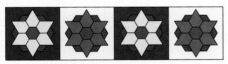

Star strip
Make 2.

10. Sew a star strip to the bottom and another to the top of the quilt centre, making sure that the background squares alternate between black and cream.

Add star strips to the top and bottom of the quilt.

11. Press. Your quilt should now measure 36½" × 36½".

SECOND BORDER

1. Stitch the 1½" × 36½" red border strips to the top and bottom of the quilt.

2. Stitch the 1½" × 38½" red border strips to the opposite sides of the quilt.

Add the border strips to the quilt.

SWAG BORDER

Using the 8½″ × 60″ cream border strips, add a mitred border to the quilt body. For information on making a mitred border, see Mitred Corner Borders (pages 29–30).

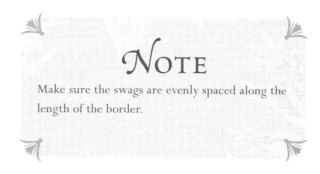

NOTE

It is important that the mitres be exact and the corners of the quilt top be square.

Swag Appliqué

1. Mark the centre lines in the cream border strips by folding them in half in both directions and pressing lightly.

2. Evenly space the swags, making sure they are centred in the width of the border.

Swag appliqué placement diagram

NOTE

Make sure the swags are evenly spaced along the length of the border.

3. Glue-baste and appliqué into position.

4. Position the fleurs-de-lis and appliqué into place.

5. Position the circles and appliqué into place.

CHECKERED BORDER

1. Stitch the remaining 3½″ × 3½″ black and cream squares together in pairs containing 1 cream square and 1 black square each.

2. Stitch 18 pairs of squares together to make a checkered strip. Make 2.

3. Press well on the right side.

4. Sew to the top and bottom of the quilt.

5. Stitch 22 pairs of squares together to make a checkered strip. Make 2.

Checkered strips

6. Press well on the right side.

7. Sew to the opposite sides of the quilt. Press.

Quilt layout diagram

Template pattern for the jewel

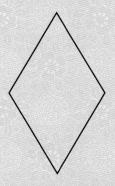

Template pattern for the diamond

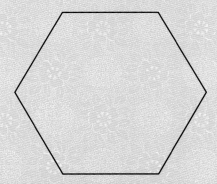

Template pattern for the hexagon

FINISHING THE QUILT

For information about how to layer, prepare for quilting, and bind your project, see Finishing Your Quilt (pages 28–32).

❋ Add a ¼" seam allowance to the fabric shapes but not to the paper shapes.

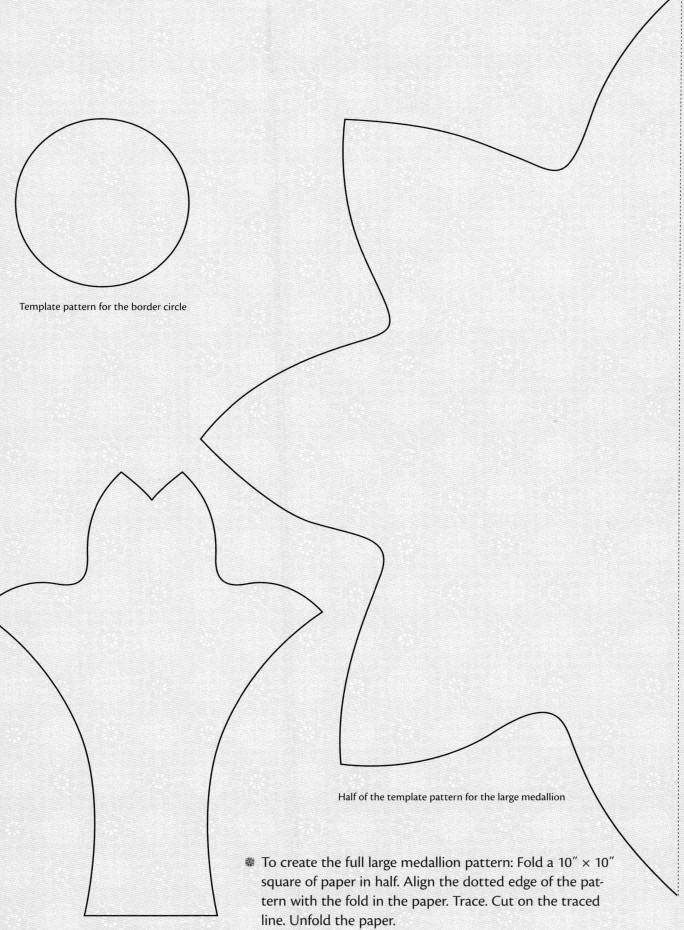

Template pattern for the border circle

Half of the template pattern for the large medallion

❋ To create the full large medallion pattern: Fold a 10″ × 10″ square of paper in half. Align the dotted edge of the pattern with the fold in the paper. Trace. Cut on the traced line. Unfold the paper.

Template pattern for the border fleur-de-lis

Template pattern for the small medallion

Template pattern for the border swag

FEATHERS & FLOWERS

Made by Sue Daley, 2010; machine quilted by Leanne Lawrence

QUILT SIZE 64" × 64" | **NUMBER OF BLOCKS** 12

ENGLISH PAPER-PIECING SHAPES

2" SCALLOPS | 2" DIAMONDS | 2" SQUARES

Material Requirements and Cutting Instructions

You will need a paper and a fabric shape for each scallop, diamond, and square in the quilt.
Use the template patterns on page 89. Add a ¼" seam allowance to each fabric piece.

For information on templates, see Making Templates (page 20).

Yardage	For	Cutting
2⅞ yards (2.6m) of 60"-wide tan print fabric	Centre block	Cut 1 square 53" × 53".
	Outside border	Cut 4 strips 6½" × 53".
	Border cornerstones	Cut 4 squares 6½" × 6½".
	Binding	Cut 5 strips 2" × the width of the fabric.
½ yard (40cm) of cream fabric	Scallops	Cut 32 scallops.
	Squares	Cut 48 squares 2½" × 2½".
¼ yard (20cm) each of 12 assorted fabrics	Scallops	Cut 6 scallops from each fabric.
	Squares	Cut 4 squares 2½" × 2½" from each fabric.
¼ yard (20cm) each of 12 assorted fabrics	Diamonds	Cut 8 diamonds from each fabric.
	Squares	Cut 1 square 2½" × 2½" from each fabric.
⅛ yard (10cm) of pink fabric	Squares	Cut 12 squares 2½" × 2½".
⅝ yard (50cm) of rust fabric	Feathers	Cut 5 centre feathers. Cut 4 corner feathers. Cut 4 corner feathers, reversed.
⅛ yard (10cm) of yellow fabric	Circles	Cut 5 circles.
¼ yard (20cm) of green fabric	Stems	Cut ½" bias strips to make about 24" in total.
	Leaves	Cut 4 leaves. Cut 4 leaves, reversed.
⅛ yard (10cm) each of 3 assorted fabrics	Flowers	Cut 8 flower centres. Cut 8 flowers. Cut 8 calyxes.
4¼ yards (3.8m) of fabric	Backing	Cut in half from selvage to selvage. Seam horizontally to make a square approximately 72" × 72".
72" × 72" of batting/wadding		

chart continued on page 85

chart continued from page 84

Yardage	For	Cutting
	Paper shapes for English paper piecing Template patterns are on page 89.	Cut 120 squares 2″ × 2″. (*Optional: 3 Patchwork with Busyfingers paper pieces packs*) Cut 96 diamonds 2″. (*Optional: 1 Busyfingers papers and template set and 1 paper pieces pack*) Cut 104 scallops 2″. (*Optional: 3 Busyfingers paper pieces packs*)

Other Requirements
Clover ¼″ bias tape maker

My love of scrappy quilts and reproduction fabrics was the inspiration for this design. This quilt was made entirely from my stash, except for the background fabric.

CONSTRUCTION TECHNIQUES

Use a ¼″ seam allowance unless stated otherwise. For information about cutting and piecing, see English Paper-Piecing Techniques (pages 14–18). To learn more about how to appliqué, see Appliqué Techniques (pages 19–27).

MAKING THE PIECED STAR BORDER

Star Blocks

1. Piece together a pair of diamonds in the same colour. Make 4.

Diamond unit
Make 4.

2. Piece together a cream square and a square in a different colour than the one you chose for the diamond sets. Make 4.

Square unit
Make 4.

3. Join 2 of the units you made in Step 2 with a square in the same fabric as the diamond units.

4. Stitch together the units you made in Steps 1–3 to make a star block. Repeat Steps 1–4 to make 12 star blocks.

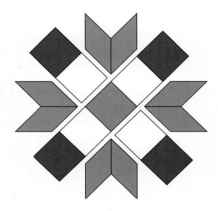

Star block
Make 12.

Assembling the Border

1. Join 3 blocks together with a pink 2″ × 2″ square between each block. Make 4 sets. For the inset seams, stitch up one seam, turn and realign, and then continue stitching.

Three-block sets
Make 4.

2. Press on the right side.

3. Arrange the block sets into a square pattern, adding 2″ × 2″ squares between the sets.

Centre star border

4. Press on the right side.

5. Mark the centre lines in the 53″ × 53″ background square by folding it in half in both directions and pressing lightly.

6. Place the square flat, right side facing up. Make sure it is nice and flat.

❧ Tip ❧

I like to place the background fabric on top of a blanket on a flat surface so it will not move while I am working on it.

7. Remove the papers from the pieced section and place it on top of the square on point, matching the centres of the corner blocks with the centre lines of the background fabric.

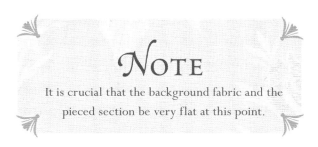

NOTE

It is crucial that the background fabric and the pieced section be very flat at this point.

Pieced section placement diagram

8. Fold back a section at a time of the pieced design and apply a small amount of appliqué glue. Continue until the whole piece is glue-basted into position.

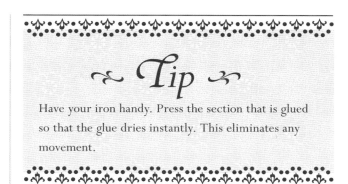

ᴖ Tip ᴖ

Have your iron handy. Press the section that is glued so that the glue dries instantly. This eliminates any movement.

9. Appliqué into position and press.

10. Using the Clover bias maker, make 4 bias strips, each 6″ long, for the flower stems. Trim each strip to the correct size when you appliqué the corner flowers. (See Bias Strip Appliqué, pages 25–26, for instructions on using the Clover bias maker.)

11. Following the appliqué placement diagram, appliqué the centre feathers and the corner flowers to the background square. Press well on the right side.

Appliqué placement diagram

12. Trim the quilt centre to 52½″ × 52½″.

MAKING THE SCALLOPED BORDER

1. Piece together 26 scallops to form a scalloped border. Make 4.

Scalloped border section
Make 4.

NOTE

Do not baste the bottom edge of the scallops over the paper shape.

2. Press well on the right side.

3. Mark the centre lines of the border strips by folding them in half in both directions and pressing lightly.

4. Remove the scallop papers and mark the centre of each pieced strip with a pin.

5. Place 1 border strip flat, right side facing up.

6. Place 1 scalloped border section on top of the border strip, right side facing up, lining up the raw edge of the scalloped section with the edge of the border strip. Match the centre of the scalloped section with the centre of the border background strip.

¼″ seam allowance

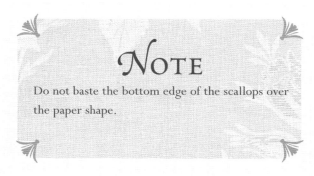

Placement diagram for the scalloped border

7. Appliqué the scalloped strip to the border. Make 4.

8. Trim the border pieces to 52½″ long.

QUILT ASSEMBLY

1. Sew border strips to opposite sides of the quilt.

2. Stitch a 6½″ × 6½″ square to each end of the 2 remaining borders.

3. Sew these borders to the top and bottom of the quilt.

4. Appliqué a flower to each corner of the quilt.

Order of placement for border corner flower

Quilt assembly diagram

FINISHING THE QUILT

For information about how to layer, prepare for quilting, and bind your project, see Finishing Your Quilt (pages 28–32).

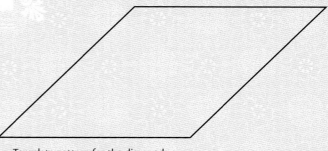

Template pattern for the diamond

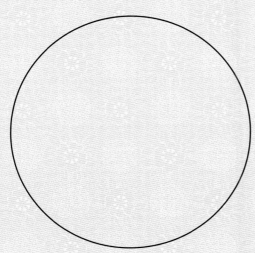

Template pattern for the circle

Template pattern for the square

(Use the square pattern for paper shapes only. Fabric squares are cut with the seam allowance added in the cutting chart.)

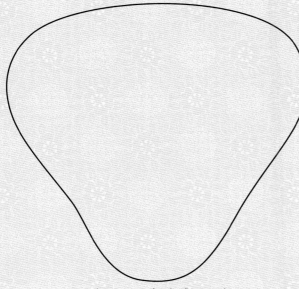

Template pattern for the flower calyx

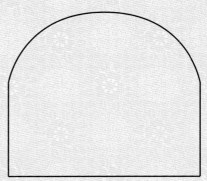

Template pattern for the scallop

✺ Add a ¼" seam allowance to the fabric shapes but not to the paper shapes.

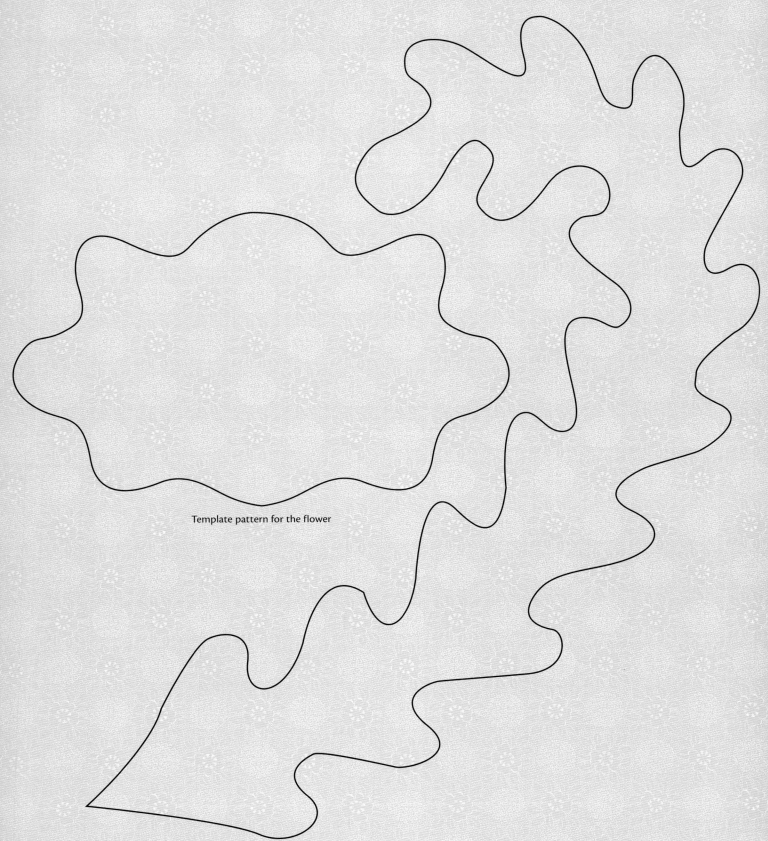

Template pattern for the flower

Template pattern for the feather in the centre block

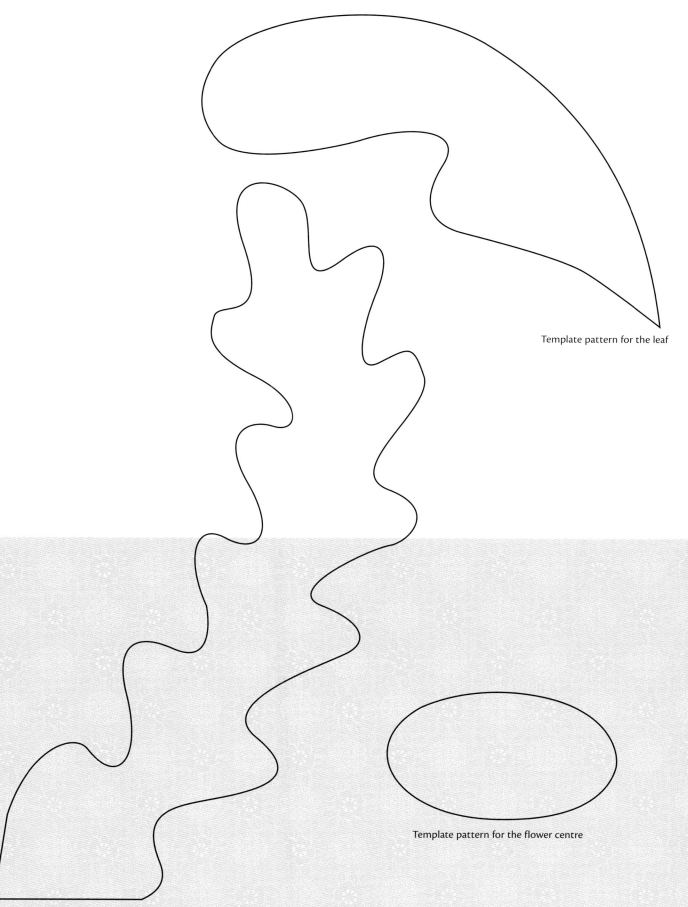

Template pattern for the leaf

Template pattern for the flower centre

Template pattern for the corner feather

ABOUT THE AUTHOR

Photo by Sandra Faye

Sue Daley was born and raised in the southern suburbs of Sydney, Australia.

She worked for many years as a detail draftsperson, but her love of fabric and design was so great that eventually it took over her life.

Her mother, Bobbie, is a beautiful embroiderer. Her grandmother Rosie was a patchworker, but it wasn't until Rosie turned 100 years old that Sue became aware of this. Rosie lived in the United Kingdom, and Sue met her only one time, in 1978. So she was not aware that they shared the same passion for patchwork. After Rosie passed away at the age of 102, Sue received a parcel in the post; much to her surprise, inside was an English paper-pieced hexagon quilt made by her grandmother.

Sue now lives on the beautiful Sunshine Coast in Queensland, Australia. When she is not travelling the world sharing her love of patchwork, Sue spends her time designing new quilt patterns and writing books for the patchwork industry.

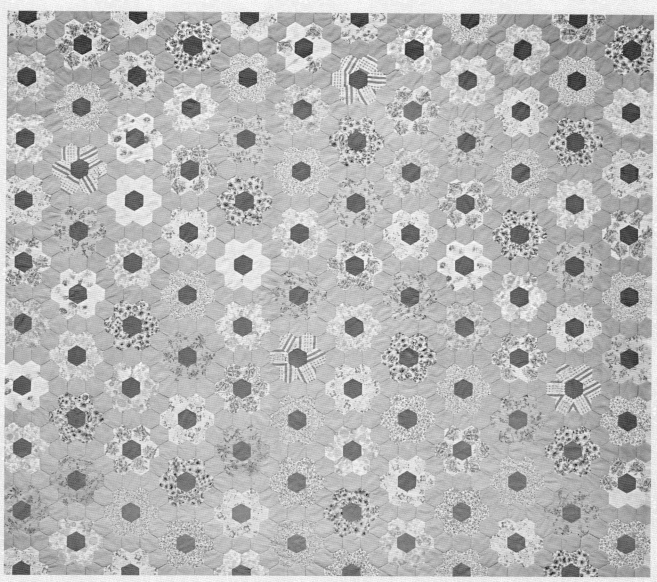

Grandma Rosie's quilt

RESOURCES

For other fine books

C&T Publishing, Inc.

www.ctpub.com

For quilting supplies

Cotton Patch

www.quiltusa.com

Patchwork with Busyfingers

www.busyfingerspatchwork.com

Products include precut papers and templates, rotating cutting boards, milliner's/straw needles, appliqué glue., and sandpaper boards.

For Superior Bottom Line thread

Superior Threads

800-499-1777

www.superiorthreads.com

For Sewline Fabric Glue Pens and refills and Sewline Trio fabric pencils

Westek Incorporated

www.sewline-product.com

For wholesale information, click on your geographic location under Distribution Agent.

Great Titles *from* C&T PUBLISHING and stashBOOKS.

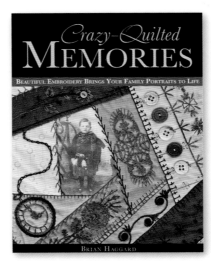

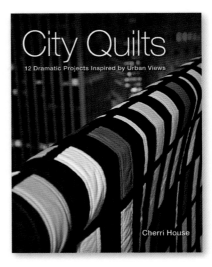

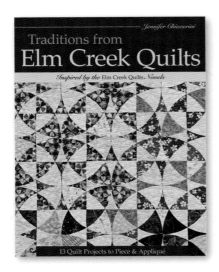

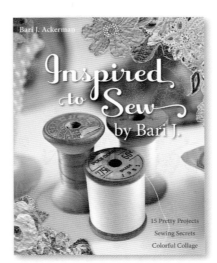

Available at your local retailer or **www.ctpub.com** *or* **800-284-1114**

*For a list of other fine books from C&T Publishing, visit our website
to view our catalogue online.*

C&T PUBLISHING, INC.
P.O. Box 1456
Lafayette, CA 94549
800-284-1114
011 + 1 + 925-677-0377

Email: ctinfo@ctpub.com
Website: www.ctpub.com

*C&T Publishing's professional photography services are now available to
the public. Visit us at www.ctmediaservices.com.*

For quilting supplies:

COTTON PATCH
1025 Brown Ave.
Lafayette, CA 94549
Store: 925-284-1177
Mail order: 925-283-7883

Email: CottonPa@aol.com
Website: www.quiltusa.com

*Note: Fabrics shown may not be currently available, as fabric
manufacturers keep most fabrics in print for only a short time.*

Tips and Techniques *can be found at www.ctpub.com > Consumer
Resources > Quiltmaking Basics: Tips & Techniques for Quiltmaking & More*